The Cry for Spiritual Fathers and Mothers is much more than a road map showing how we who are mature Christians must nurture the newer generations. It is all of that, but it is also an awesome word for cutting-edge leadership in today's church. I, for one, want to be the kind of a fatherly leader that Larry Kreider urges us to be.

—C. Peter Wagner, Chancellor, Wagner Leadership Institute

The Cry for Spiritual Fathers and Mothers brilliantly explains what it means to be a mentor in the body of Christ. Insights are both biblical and practical...an important book for those desiring to effectively equip believers for ministry. Larry has captured the very heart of kingdom principles in this book. It is a classic that you will want to read with a highlighter pen!

—Dr. Ralph Neighbour Jr., Touch Ministries, Houston, Texas

There are a few significant books on my bookshelf about the important issue of spiritual fathering and mothering, but none of them tops this one. Larry Kreider has reached into the storehouse of his unique experience and insight to offer us what will no doubt become a new standard on the subject. Because Larry's understanding of the role of spiritual parents in the family of God is so profound, I enthusiastically recommend this book to you.

—Dr. David Cannistraci, Evangel Christian Fellowship, San Jose, California

The Cry for Spiritual Fathers and Mothers comes like a drink of cold water to the thirsty. So many people, including ministers, have been fatherless and left disconnected. I believe this book will answer one of the greatest needs in the body of Christ today. The anointing of God upon this book is because of the anointing of God upon Larry Kreider. This apostolic father has been such a friend and an inspiration. This book will deeply touch your life. Reading it will be like a child who has been searching for a father, finally being lifted in the arms of his heavenly Father and sitting on His lap.

—Pastor Sam Hinn, The Gathering Place Worship Center, Orlando, Florida

Larry Kreider has identified the key issue in the church world today. Will the church become a parenting force to impart health to a broken world? The implications of the spirit of fathering affect every area of personal and corporate spiritual life. There is an urgent call today for relationships that provide healthy spiritual nurture and authority. God is calling us to actively give ourselves to both being spiritually fathered as well as becoming spiritual fathers. Larry Kreider not only teaches on spiritual fathering, he is a spiritual father—and through his words, the Lord calls us to maturity.

—Robert Stearns, founder and director of Eagles's Wings Ministries

In a world where "individual rights" often overshadow "individual responsibility," Larry Kreider's *The Cry for Spiritual Fathers and Mothers* reaffirms God's divine order. Having known Larry for almost 20 years, I have seen firsthand how his life embodies his message. Following the example of Jesus, Larry "did" before he "taught," and spiritually fathered thousands of young men and women. May this book open your eyes to become a spiritual parent to this next generation.

—Francis Anfuso, Senior Pastor, The Rock of Roseville, Roseville, California

Larry Kreider is probably one of the most fathering guys I have ever met. He has the ability to combine the spiritual and the practical in his life and ministry. Wisdom and life flow freely as he invites us into the security and release that spiritual fathering brings. The source and the spirit of this book flow from the very heart of the Father. The message is timely and desperately needed. I highly recommend it.

—Alan Platt, Senior Pastor, Doxadeo, Pretoria, South Africa

The Cry for Spiritual Fathers and Mothers is a timely word to the body of Christ. There is an urgent need in this hour for the hearts of spiritual parents and spiritual children to be restored to one another. The words on these pages are more than theories. They are life-style. I have seen Larry and LaVerne live these truths. The fruit of their ministry is obvious. So, embrace the challenge. Receive the grace for your parental ministry. Let's so live our lives that Paul would have to say: "You not only have many teachers. You also have many fathers!"

—Pastor Dave Hess, Christ Community Church, Camp Hill, Pennsylvania

Larry Kreider's book, *The Cry for Spiritual Fathers and Mothers,* reflects the values and vision he has imparted to DOVE Christian Fellowship International. The wisdom of these pages shows why DOVE has produced a stable, growing apostolic stream. When many American movements have declined or disappeared, Larry shows the way to growth and stability in spiritual fathering.

—Dr. Daniel C. Juster, International Director, Tikkun International

Larry shares his autobiography as a spiritual parent including many practical applications from the context of small group ministry. He sounds a passionate call with compelling vision for us all to enlist as spiritual fathers and mothers.

—Keith Yoder, Ed. D., Director of Teaching the Word Ministries, Leola, PA.

As you know how we exhorted, and comforted,
and charged every one of you, as a
father does his own children, that you would have a
walk worthy of God who
calls you into His own kingdom and glory.
I Thessalonians 2:11-12

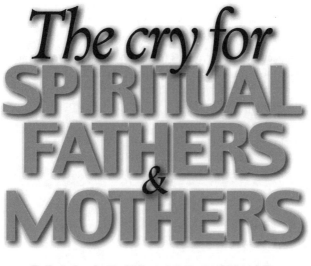

The cry for SPIRITUAL FATHERS & MOTHERS

BY LARRY KREIDER

House to House Publications
1924 West Main Street • Ephrata, PA 17522

Some of the anecdotal illustrations in this book are true to life and are included with the permission of the persons involved. All other illustrations are composites of real situations, and any resemblance to people living or dead is coincidental.

ISBN 1-886973-42-3

First Printing, June 2000
Second Printing, December 2000

Unless otherwise noted, all scripture quotations in this publication are taken from the New King James Version (NKJV) of the Bible, © 1979, 1980, 1982, Thomas Nelson Inc.

Printed in the United States of America

Dedication

This book is affectionately dedicated to my wife LaVerne,
my partner in both natural and spiritual parenting,

to my godly parents, Harold and Esther Kreider,
and parents-in-law, Parke and Charity Heller
for your loving parenting for the past 50 years,

to our children Katrina, Charita, Joshua, Leticia,
along with our son-in-law, David, and grandson, Connor Logan,
who have brought us great joy,

to those in the DOVE Christian Fellowship International
family of churches and ministries who have faithfully imparted what
the Lord gave them into spiritual sons and daughters,

and to our Lord Jesus Christ who is our supreme model
for spiritual fathering and mothering.

Acknowledgments

A special word of thanks must go to Karen Ruiz, my editor, who tirelessly helped me to write and rewrite this manuscript.

I also wish to express my appreciation to the DOVE Christian Fellowship International Apostolic Council and administrator, Hank Rogers, who covered for me by giving me the time I needed to write.

A number of people have been kind enough to read the manuscript for this book, and I have profited greatly from their corrections and suggestions. These include: Jackie Bowser, Peter Bunton, Carl Good, LaVerne Kreider, Shirley Hampton, Nelson Martin, Sarah Mohler, Ron Myer, Diane Omondi, Jim Pesce, Steve Prokopchak, Brian Sauder, Will Stoltzfus, Mike Stoltzfus, Barry Wissler, Stephanie Yarberough and Keith Yoder. To proofreaders, Carolyn Sprague and Jenn Lentz, thank you.

And thank you, to all who shared their stories of spiritual fathering and mothering.

Contents

Foreword

I have waited a long time for this book. There is not another one like it anywhere. *The Cry for Spiritual Fathers and Mothers* blends sound teaching on how to develop each member of the church for ministry, with spiritual fathering and mothering at every level of the church, all the while honoring the role of the senior pastor. Larry Kreider does this in the context of "every member" ministry in small groups. What pastor wouldn't want every member of his church engaged in using their spiritual gifts for effective ministry? Because *The Cry for Spiritual Fathers and Mothers* addresses such an important subject, it should be required reading for the staff and small group leaders of every local church that is becoming or has become a small group or cell-based church.

The Cry for Spiritual Fathers and Mothers addresses many of the leadership issues pastors face in discipling church members and raising up emerging leaders, and does so from a firm foundation of biblical truth. What we don't need is another book on spiritual leadership filled with anecdotes but void of scriptural principle. This book avoids that temptation. Larry combines encouraging, down to earth, helpful illustrations in every chapter, and he does this with plenty of scriptural references. This book allows us to know what Larry believes and why he believes it.

Chapter Two on reclaiming spiritual families is worth the price of the book. Larry reminds us that churches are only as effective as the relational ties the church members have with each other. And then he goes on to demonstrate how to build that kind of church.

Chapter Four, "Understanding What It Takes to Be a Father" will set the standard for leadership in your church or ministry. By taking staff members and small group leaders through an in-depth study of this chapter, a leader will save himself many heartaches. It helps build a common framework for what people can expect from their leaders, what leaders should expect from one another, and how to raise up father-leaders. This chapter, and the one on hindrances to spiritual fathering, will help define how leadership works and what to do when leaders fail for your church or ministry.

While affirming the need for spiritual fathers and mothers, Larry avoids the excesses of spiritual control and top-down church life. He believes, and demonstrates repeatedly, that when the "believer-priests" are mobilized to use their gifts, a struggling local church is transformed into a New Testament local-church.

After thirty-two years of missions work, I was looking for a book like this one to recommend to the church I now pastor. Our church is becoming a cell church with a passion to reach our city and the nations of the earth. I am committed to helping our church do five things well: inspire all those we touch to love Jesus passionately; celebrate community and love one another in outward focused small groups; equip and mobilize each person in our church for gift-based ministry; share the gospel as market place missionaries with our friends and neighbors; spread His glory to the nations as we plant churches among the least evangelized peoples of the earth.

As a pastor with a vision for our people to be involved in effective, small group ministry, I want them to catch Larry Kreider's vision for spiritual fathering and mothering. As Larry has so effectively communicated in his book, spiritual parenting is something every person can do. When the saints believe this, and when we as leaders are focused with single-minded determination to see it become a reality, it will happen. Then God will have a people for Himself that reflects His glory.

A book that helps us know how to go about raising up spiritual fathers and mothers, while warning us of the pitfalls and dangers along the way, is invaluable. I devoured Larry's book in one reading, and now I want to go back and digest it so I can pass on to others what I have learned. I hope you will do the same.

—Floyd McClung
April, 2000
Kansas City, Missouri

Introduction

J ust as the prophet Malachi cried out that Elijah would come to "turn the hearts of the fathers to their children" there is a cry ringing out for spiritual fathers and mothers today. People are longing for spiritual relationships that are connected, fulfilling and real.

I know what the need for a spiritual father feels like. I served as a pastor for fifteen years in Lancaster County, Pennsylvania, USA. During this time, we experienced tremendous blessings from the Lord. Our church of twenty-five people grew to more than 2,300 believers within ten years. It all looked great on the surface. Yet deep in my heart, I was longing for a spiritual father—someone I could just sit down with and talk to, someone with whom I could be entirely open and honest concerning the questions that I had and the problems I was facing.

Joshua had Moses, Elisha had Elijah, Ruth had Naomi, and Timothy had Paul. I felt like I had no one. I knew that if God's people were to prosper spiritually, my generation had to endeavor to pour what we had into the next generation by imparting to them our "fatherhood." At the same time, we had to trust God to provide spiritual fathers and mothers for us.

Today, I am a blessed man. As I have taken a step of faith to become a spiritual father to others, the Lord has brought spiritual fathers into my life. *The Cry For Spiritual Fathers and Mothers* comes out of what I have learned personally during my own pilgrimage in spiritual parenting and from what I have learned from others I have come to respect as spiritual fathers and mothers.

This is a book telling how the heart of a spiritual parent can be turned to their spiritual children. It is a book for those in the "here and now" who want to look with satisfaction at the future—envisioning their spiritual posterity stretched out into infinity.

This is not another book on discipleship. Discipleship most often implies two people getting together for a structured, "precept upon precept" method of helping a young Christian become a well-disciplined soldier of Christ. These kinds of relationships certainly are needed and are wonderful vehicles to train believers, but discipleship does not quite encompass the scope of spiritual fathering and mothering.

Spiritual fathering and mothering is perhaps best expressed through the term *mentoring*. Mentoring communicates the key ideas of the process of spiritual fathering and mothering because it has an intention of servanthood to develop and encourage people as they walk the path of becoming spiritual fathers and mothers themselves.

If, at places throughout the book, I use the term spiritual father without referring to mothers, I do so to make the text easier to read. Spiritual fathering is not gender-specific. Women are not excluded from wider mentoring roles in the body of Christ. There is a desperate need for spiritual mothers in the church of Jesus Christ today.

My prayer is that you may discover how the heart of fathers and mothers can be turned to their children and be challenged, refreshed and changed by the Holy Spirit as you prayerfully read through the pages of this book.

—Larry Kreider
International Director
DOVE Christian Fellowship Int'l
1924 West Main Street
Ephrata, Pennsylvania 17522

CHAPTER 1

Wanted: Spiritual Fathers and Mothers

Why we need them so desperately

I was traveling with a well-known evangelist in the nation of New Zealand and had just experienced listening to his powerful preaching a few hours before. It was electrifying! As we sat in the back of a van driving down a scenic New Zealand road between meetings, he said something that I will never forget. He turned to me with a tired, almost wistful quality in his voice and said, "Larry, you know what I really need? I need a father."

I admit, I was temporarily speechless. Here was a powerfully anointed leader, highly successful as an evangelist, whose greatest need was for someone who cared deeply and could interact with him and help sort out nagging questions when he ran into problems. He was longing for a spiritual father from whom he could receive an imprint—a seasoned older man to encourage him and give him positive feedback.

A new Christian stopped by our house one day, depressed and discouraged. "Larry and LaVerne," she said to my wife and me, "I know the Lord has changed my life, but there is so much I don't understand. I'm not sure if I'll make it. Our pastor uses 'thousand dollar words,' and I just can't decipher what they mean." Then she admitted the true cry of her heart, "I really need someone to help me understand the things I'm taught. I need a spiritual mom to help me grow up spiritually."

An elderly pastor was ready to retire and hand the baton over to the younger leadership. He nearly wept as he confided in me that he felt dishonored by the leaders he had trained to take his place. He admitted that he somehow missed the mark when it came to training and raising his spiritual sons. They did not honor him as a spiritual father.

Encounters like these, with spiritual sons and daughters who yearn for spiritual moms and dads, and spiritual fathers who tried unsuccessfully to pass on a legacy of spiritual fatherhood to the next generation, paint a clear picture of a present day reality in the church. God has created us with a need to feel connected in relationships but a painful lack of nurturing, support and interaction has created a void between the generations.

As I travel throughout the world, training leaders and potential leaders week after week, I see a consistent and desperate need for spiritual fathers and mothers to be in vital relationships with spiritual children. Whether they are new believers, Christians for many years, or pastors, the need is still the same. Deep down inside, many are longing for spiritual fathers and mothers.

More and more believers are awakening to the need. Currently, in our county in Pennsylvania, there is a powerful move of God among young people. It started when a few youth got serious about reaching their peers for Christ. The Bible study they started now has more than 1,000 kids attending every Tuesday night. One of the young leaders told me why he felt the Lord chose our area for a move of God: "We had spiritual fathers here who were ready and willing to serve and encourage us."

When spiritual fathers pour what the Lord has given them into spiritual sons and daughters, the resulting relationships will produce children who respect and honor their parents and are prepared to become spiritual parents for the next generation.

People need "anchoring"

All humanity begs for authentic relationships, both in the church and in the world. Too often, a fractured family life has cheated people out of the real relationships that give people security. That is why we see a growing trend in today's society to reclaim spiritual roots and family.

America's number one talk show host, Oprah Winfrey, daily invites people to share their stories of redemption and rediscovery of spiritual values and relationships that help them connect in a disconnected world. Parents want their children to seek spiritual guidance and find protection in successful relationships so they do not have to face an increasingly hostile world alone.

I was amazed recently to read an airline magazine article telling of a secular futurist's predictions of trends in American society. Apparently, Faith Popcorn and her consulting company, New York City-based BrainReserve, provide advice about future consumer trends—how subtle social and demographic changes can create opportunities for product changes that anticipate consumer demand. BrainReserve has a talent bank of 5,000 people globally who are experts in just about everything imaginable. Ms. Popcorn has been remarkably accurate in her predictions and trends (among them the failure of "New Coke" and the popularity of sport utility vehicles).

Ms. Popcorn has recently coined the word "anchoring" for the next trend in society she sees emerging. Here's what she has to say: "It's a spiritual thing. The trend is clear. You see it in movies—The Prince of Egypt, City of Angels, The Apostle. And in books: *Chicken Soup for the Soul, Conversations with God, Talking to Heaven.*"

She believes people are scared—school-yard violence, technological advances leading to a lack of privacy, pornography at the click of a computer mouse, senseless crime—all of this "makes society hungry and desperate for guidance and moral authority."[1] I have to agree with her. People are looking for direction in today's world. They are searching for spiritual answers more than ever before. And they want real relationships where they can feel connected and safe.

God will turn the hearts of fathers to children

God's intention is to raise up spiritual parents who are willing to nurture spiritual children and help them grow up in their Christian lives. This is a fulfillment of the Lord's promise in the last days to "turn the hearts of the fathers to the children, and the hearts of the children to their fathers..." (Malachi 4:6).

The Lord wants to restore harmony among fathers and their children, both naturally and spiritually, so fathers can freely impart their inheritance to the next generation. He wants spiritual fathers and mothers to take up the mantle to train their children so they no longer flounder in the sea of life. Children need to have the kind of parents in their lives providing the character they need, telling them they are valuable, that they are gifts from God. Parents need to put expectation into children's hearts so that they believe in themselves.

With the old and the young working together, a mighty and ongoing spiritual legacy will multiply and endure. Imparting spiritual fatherhood fills the void and closes the gap of broken relationships between the old and the young.

Too often, in today's church, a Christian believer is encouraged to participate in church services, Bible studies, para-church organizations or evangelistic ministry in order to bolster his faith and "grow strong in the Lord." The theory is that the more teaching from God's Word and interaction with believers, the more spiritually mature he will become. As important as these involvements may be, such a faulty supposition leads to inhaling message after message, book after book, tape after tape, seminar after seminar in order to fill a void for real relationship.

A believer becomes fat spiritually and fails to interpret what he is learning so he can pass it on to others. He does not know how to meaningfully and sacrificially impart his life to others because he has never been properly fathered. Without a role model, he remains a spiritual infant, needing to be spoon-fed by his pastor or other Christian worker.

"You do not have many fathers"

Paul, the apostle, warned the Corinthian church not to overlook the need to make lasting spiritual investments in others' lives as spiritual fathers. "For though you might have ten thousand instructors in Christ, yet you do not have many fathers; for in Christ Jesus I have begotten you through the gospel" (I Corinthians 4:15).

The Greek word for *instructor* in this verse refers to one who is responsible for the supervision of children until they reach adulthood. It seems Paul was challenging the Corinthian church that they had many baby-sitters or schoolteachers in their spiritual lives, but he was the only one who "fathered" them into that life. As a concerned father, Paul had their best interests at heart.

Since the time Paul had brought them to faith in Christ, many instructors had subsequently taught God's Word to the Corinthians. They heard these instructors, faithfully attended church services, but became "puffed up" (verse 18) in their knowledge of the gospel. They were proud of what they knew, but they were immature as believers because they lacked true fathers to give them an identity and proper training and nurturing. This created a dilemma. They did not have spiritual fathers who were willing to pass on a legacy to their spiritual children.

Paul modeled spiritual fathering

That's why Paul says in verse 17 that he is going to send Timothy to the Corinthian church because he would "remind you of my way of life in Christ Jesus." As a spiritual father, Paul faithfully trained Timothy. Now Timothy was ready to impart *his* spiritual fatherhood to the Corinthian church. Christian believers need to see spiritual fathering modeled so they can be equipped to pass on a legacy to the next generation of believers.

To find their way out of this dilemma, Paul reminds the Corinthian church of the truth of fatherhood. He trained Timothy, his beloved and trustworthy spiritual son, and now Timothy was coming to train them. Paul trusted Timothy to help the wayward Corinthian church because Paul had trained him like a son. With this example, they would soon be producing their own spiritual sons and daughters. This kind of mentoring relationship of training and equipping sons and daughters was a spiritual investment that could continue to multiply.

Paul knew that in order for the church to grow spiritually, each believer must be in vital relationships with others who had gone down this spiritual road before; otherwise they would be content to do what the "instructors" told them to do rather than learning how to hear from God themselves as they received mentoring from a loving spiritual father.

The struggle for identity

As God's people, we need help to grow up. It is very difficult to do it by ourselves, just as natural infants cannot thrive if left on their own. Babies need the care and nurture of parents just as believers need the practical input from loving fathers who delight in their children reaching their full potential in Christ. *of orphans in Romania*

It was the lack of mature leadership in the Corinthian church that stunted the believers' spiritual growth. Unequipped to grow up spiritually, they struggled to find their identity. They did not know who they were in the Lord.

When believers lack spiritual fathers or mothers to model God's fatherhood, they often struggle, feeling spiritually alone and without an identity. Because they did not have their identity in Christ, the Corinthians sought it through their favorite leader: "'I am of Paul,' and another, 'I am of Apollos...'" (I Corinthians 3:4). Paul chides the Corinthian church for its lack of maturity making it plain that, while people have a role to play, it is clearly only God who is the source of any good thing, and it is only Him whom they should ultimately follow. Deficient of true spiritual fathers to model fatherhood, the Corinthian church had become a system that produced programs and teachers, but they were not producing sons and daughters.

What they really needed were spiritual fathers and mothers to pay close attention to them so they could be nudged toward maturity. They needed spiritual parents to sow into their lives, expecting them eventually to become spiritual parents themselves. The goal was to create a spiritual harvest that would continue to multiply. An investment like this pays off great dividends!

A spiritual investment

Wouldn't it be great if someone saw your potential in Christ and decided to invest in your life? What do you think would happen if more Christians made themselves available in spiritual fathering relationships?

My friend Don Finto, who served as the senior pastor of Belmont Church in Nashville, Tennessee for many years, has a great passion to father younger men in ministry. I recently discovered this interesting bit of information about his relationship with one of his more famous "spiritual sons," the singer and musician, Michael W. Smith:

> For the last 20 years—starting before Smith cut any records—Finto has laughed, cried, worshiped, prayed and traveled together with Smith in a father-son type of relationship.
>
> "I could write a book about Finto," Smith says. "He's my daddy in the Lord. I don't think I'd be where I am today if it hadn't been for Don."
>
> Finto now serves as a pastor to pastors. "I am an encour-

ager," Finto admits. "I can often see more in people than they can see in themselves, and I want to call it forth in the name of the Lord."

The effect of his ministry gift on Smith has been profound. "I've saved all my letters from him, all the little note cards," Smith says. "He has encouraged me in so many ways—my self-confidence and who I am in the Lord—pulling stuff out of me that nobody ever was able to pull out." [2]

We need to see many more scenarios like this become common-place so that spiritual fathering can be restored. The potential for spiritual fathering is truly enormous.

Geese fly in a "V" formation because the aerodynamics of the "V" enable the geese to fly over seventy percent further than if they fly alone. As each bird flaps its wings, an updraft is created for the bird behind it. When the bird in front gets tired, he moves back in the formation. Geese go a lot further when they work together. That is the point of a spiritual fathering relationship—we can go a lot further spiritually if we work together in family-like units to reach the world.

Understanding the differences between generations

With the peaceful working together of inter-generational families, a blessing is passed on from one generation to the next. When the hearts of the children and the fathers are turned toward each other rather than against each other, we create an environment that allows individuals and teams to give their best. This working relationship is a challenge for today's mix of generations. It does not just happen.

Recently I read a review of the book *Generations at Work*, which gives a profile of today's generational personalities. I am including it here because I believe it can help us in understanding the context that gave rise to each generation's values and ideas. Knowing the whole picture helps us to embrace each other as we relate in spiritual fathering relationships in the church:

The Veterans (born 1922-1943) value the dedication and sacrifice they witnessed during WWII, and the hard work, conformity and respect for authority that permeated corporate culture in the '50s. The Boomers (1943-1960), on the other hand, grew up questioning authority and believing that "anything is possible." They're passionate workaholics, optimistic, team oriented and interested in personal growth and involvement. The Gen Xers (1960-1980) were latchkey children (their boomer parents were at work all the time), and while they became self-reliant out of necessity, they also developed a good deal of cynicism. They are determined to live more balanced lives than their elders—"It's just a job" is their motto. Still, they like solving problems and getting things done, as long as they can do things their way. The Nexters (1980-2000), on the cusp of entering the workforce, identify most with the Veterans—loyal, hardworking and respectful of authority.[3]

Today's world and church is filled with a blend of generations that must learn how to work together. Understanding the values and needs of each generation helps us to understand each other.

Multigenerational situations within the family and church are bound to generate conflicts. Tensions can be lessened when each spiritual father and son, and spiritual mother and daughter, determines to use his or her strengths to help each other's weaknesses.

Every believer, young and old, is important and useful in God's kingdom. Spiritual fathering relationships provide a powerful avenue of involvement for everyone. This great mix of generations needs to learn to understand each other, accept each other and forgive each other as they work toward building healthy relationships.

Let's not lose the harvest

We live in exciting days in the history of the church. I believe we are on the verge of a great end-time harvest. Just as God magnetically drew the animals to Noah's ark, He is drawing multitudes of people to Himself in these last days. Statistics show us that the ratio of people being saved today compared to twenty years ago is escalating. Clearly, the wind of the Holy Spirit is sweeping our world in an unprecedented manner.

In the next years as we race toward the last chapter in history, we need to prepare for hundreds of thousands of souls coming into the kingdom of God in our communities. A great harvest is promised, and it is sure to come (Revelation 7:9). We must continue to prepare and be ready to care for the harvest when it pours in.

I grew up on a farm. I know that various crops are ready to be harvested at different times of the year. We had to be alert, with our barns and equipment ready, so we could harvest our crops at just the right time to reap a good harvest. Jesus, Himself, tells us to be constantly alert and ready. "Do you not say, 'There are still four months and then comes the harvest'? Behold, I say to you, lift up your eyes and look at the fields, for they are already white for harvest!" (John 4:35).

Down through the ages, the Lord has continually drawn people to Himself as many souls were harvested into His kingdom. Sometimes, however, a large portion of the harvest was lost because Christians were not alert and ready.

It seems to me that one such huge harvest for which the church was not prepared occurred in the late 1960's to mid 1970's. It was called the "Jesus People Movement." This movement began when a number of believers in Christ entered the hippie counterculture community and shared the gospel of Jesus Christ with them, resulting in a massive number of conversions to Christianity among young people. By early 1971, there were Jesus People coffeehouses, communes and other types of establishments in every state and province across the United States and Canada.

But much of the church was unprepared for this radical new breed of Christians. The tension between the Jesus People and the established churches was a source of irritation for the Jesus People who saw the church as slow-moving and steeped in tradition and legalism. The church often could not understand these kids with long hair and sandals. Although some churches and Christian communities did welcome these new converts with open arms and disciple them, many new believers fell by the wayside and were disillusioned.

Calling all spiritual fathers and mothers

If the church had been prepared and had more understanding of these young people during this huge revival, I believe the harvest could have been much greater. In my opinion, there were simply not enough spiritual fathers and mothers willing to put their arms around these "Jesus freaks" and nurture them as babes in Christ until they could stand on their own. May we not make the same mistake in this generation! The Lord is calling for thousands of spiritual fathers and mothers to be willing to prepare now for the coming harvest.

The devil, from the time of Adam on, has fought the truth of spiritual parenting because it is a story of the restoration of relationships with God and with man. All hell comes against this powerful truth because Satan knows that if any generation really believes in and practices the principle of spiritual fathering—the kingdom of God will burst forth in power unlike any time in history.

We need to pray for all spiritual fathers and mothers to stand up and be counted. When they do, God's people will discover their identities and fulfill their purpose in the kingdom of God. Join me as we learn how spiritual families can be restored so that fathers and sons, and mothers and daughters can live in connected, joyous, and fruitful relationships with each other.

Notes
[1] Robert Deitz, "Faith in the Future," *Southwest Airlines Spirit*, October 1999, p.26.
[2] "The Man Behind Michael," *Charisma Magazine*, April 2000.
[3] Amy Robinson, "Closing the Generation Gap," *Continental,* November 1999, p.74.

CHAPTER 2

Young Bull Elephants

Reclaiming spiritual family connections

W hat happens to children who are left to their own resources and are not provided with intimate family interaction and care? This story describes a possible striking chain of events:

A nationally syndicated columnist with the Washington Post recently wrote about the plight of the white rhinoceros in Pilanesberg Park, a South African game preserve. At least 39 of these endangered rhinos had been found slaughtered in their native habitat, and it was assumed that poachers were the killers of the remarkable beasts. However, upon closer inspection it was discovered that all of the rhinos' valuable horns remained among the carcasses. In an effort to catch the killers, the game wardens decided to tranquilize some of the remaining animals to electronically tag and track them. Hidden video cameras were also set in strategic locations to record the evidence.

The game wardens were amazed to discover that young bull elephants were harassing the rhinos without provocation. Although unnatural for them, these teenaged elephants were chasing these white rhinos for long distances, throwing sticks at them and stomping them to death. Why were these elephants acting so violently? The answer would be found in a decision made 20 years earlier.

Because the Kruger National Park was unable to support a continuously increasing population of elephants, park officials had decided to transport some of them to the Pilanesberg Preserve. The elephants too large to transport were killed, including a significant number of mature bulls. As a result, the elephants that were guilty of killing the rhinos matured without the influence and presence of mature males. Park rangers and scientists discovered that without the older presence of mature bulls, these young male elephants were suffering from excessive testosterone and becoming increasingly violent.

To preserve the white rhino population, park officials killed five of the most aggressive young bull elephants while determining to find a suitable answer for this aberration of nature. Park rangers decided to import older bulls in order to view their influence on the remaining young males. The young bulls learned quickly that they were no match for the more mature elephants. The older bulls began to assume their place among the herd as fathers and disciplinarians.

The younger, aggressive bulls could no longer impose their unchallenged, immature bullying. Eventually the young bulls began following the older ones. It became apparent that they enjoyed these new relationships with the older, more mature males. The former lawbreakers yielded to the new discipline and returned to normal patterns of elephant behavior. There has not been a report of any dead rhinos since the arrival of the more mature elephants.

This is a parable of life in the church. The absence of mature leadership in the church results in similar consequences. When mature Christian men and women do not assume their responsibility, the younger, more energetic and yet immature ones take their places. These leaders are not equipped for the task that lies before them.

However, if we are faithful to fulfill God's call, He will use our faithfulness to help preserve the lives of many young men and women whom God has chosen to save, deliver, and train as leaders in His household. We have seen anointed and gifted young men and woman start their walk with the Lord only to fall along the wayside, trapped by the many snares of the enemy. God is calling spiritual mothers and fathers who will arise, enter the harvest, and live for those for whom the Lord has died.[1]

The story of the rhinos reminds me of a similar dilemma Eli faced in raising his sons. Eli was a priest and father in the house of the Lord, but I Samuel 2:12 records that Eli's sons were wicked men, having no regard for the Lord. Why? Eli was lax in his discipline and training of his sons, and they became rebellious. The Lord rebuked Eli for not training his sons in the ways of the Lord. Because of this, Eli lost his family. No one would grow old in his household.

God's intention of fatherhood

What is God's plan for His people? It is for them to be His "family." *Family* is God's idea because He ordained and designed it: "I will be a Father to you, and you shall be My sons and daughters, says the Lord Almighty" (II Corinthians 6:18). God is the Father of an entire great family which includes all those who name Jesus Christ as Lord.

Paul the apostle's affectionate prayer for his beloved Ephesians states, "For this reason I bow my knees to the Father of our Lord Jesus Christ, from whom the whole family in heaven and earth is named" (Ephesians 3:14). God is the Father from whom all fatherhood derives its meaning and inspiration. We have to understand His fatherhood— His love, forgiveness and acceptance—if we are to understand healthy family relationships.

Unfortunately, today's generation has a warped understanding of fatherhood because fathers have often abused their authority or have been absent, causing a breach of trust and security. With poor role models in the world, God's people, the church of Jesus Christ, must start to model an example of God's intention for *family.*

"The church must begin to understand its role as a parenting influence—as a holistic life-growth community," says my friend Robert Stearns in his book *Prepare the Way.* "God will lead many men who have the father's heart to begin to mentor young men in their congregations...older women will take younger under their wings and impart love, nurture and wisdom. Strong families will reach out to single-parent homes and welcome ongoing interaction between the families, bringing strength and combating the overwhelming sense of 'aloneness.' We will move toward the joy that the early church exuded as they lived in fellowship with each other and the Lord."[2]

No longer can we live independently of each other. God wants to restore fathering and mothering to the kingdom of God, and it starts with His promise to be a Father to us. But for believers to experience true spiritual family life, spiritual fathers and mothers must obey the Lord's call to spiritual parenting. Families need fathers and mothers who will assume their responsibility as spiritual parents.

A spiritual father is like a natural father

The importance of fathers in a family is to bring strength, stability and balance to the family. A natural father is meant to be a protector, counselor, and guide to his children. Natural children are envisioned to grow up secure in their father's love and guidance. If they lack a healthy father role model, these children cannot achieve their destiny. According to Dr. David Cannistraci, healthy fathering is essential to success at every level of society:

> Sociologists are now confirming that fathers not only play an indispensable role in the home, but also in the nation. Many of the problems we face in America today—drugs, welfare, teenage pregnancy—are directly related to the absence of fathers throughout the past several decades.

> Fatherlessness is the most destructive trend in our generation. The absence of fathers is linked to most social nightmares. Social scientists have made similar links between a father's absence and his child's likelihood of being a dropout, jobless, a drug addict, a suicide victim, mentally ill and a target of child sexual abuse.

The strength of a father provides tremendous protection for a family's future and ultimate destiny. Spiritual fatherlessness is a weakness in the body of Christ today; a great vacuum has been created by the scarcity of godly fathering. Like society, the church is plagued with problems. We need the same kind of discipline and accountability a natural father brings to a natural family. We need wisdom and maturity, a firm hand to guide us, balance to preserve us and experience to comfort us. Noted pastor and author Frank Damazio laments the current crisis of fatherlessness permeating the body of Christ. "Today young leaders search desperately for models they can imitate and look up to. Today's leaders live when heroes have flaws and fail and when dreams have died. When religious systems are corrupt and modern ministry does not offer a mentoring model, young leaders may end up following wrong models. Without spiritual fathers, the church cannot achieve its ultimate destiny."[3]

The curse of deadbeat dads

Statistics today show a society with an alarming trend toward the deterioration of the family. Marriages are failing, parents are absent, and children are paying the emotional, financial, physical and spiritual consequences. The term for absentee dads who neglect their children is "deadbeat dads." It is not a very flattering term, but when you think of vulnerable children without an involved father, it is an accurate portrayal. The family unit has been torn apart leaving the children unprotected and drifting.

A popular view some years ago was that external forces like street crime, bad schools and economic stress were the culprits of the crisis in family life. Today's critics challenge this view. The revised thinking is that it is the breakdown of families that feeds social ills. A *U.S. News and World Report* feature article laments the damage done when selfish parents divorce and children are left to cope: "Nearly 2 of every 5 kids in America do not live with their fathers" the article reads. "Fatherlessness is the most destructive trend of our generation."[4] It went on to show the great need for reconnecting dads to their children.

Ken Canfield says it this way,

> "The psalmist cursed the evil households with fatherlessness (Psalm 109:9) because in the ancient Near East the father provided protection from the world. While many voices are crying out that we need more government to protect our families, the church is responding to a different voice—the voice of a Father. God has revealed Himself as our Father, and He is calling fathers within the church to follow His example. In this age of fatherlessness, that call to 'restore the hearts of the fathers to their children' has never been more urgent."[5]

Restoring a sense of responsibility

If the hearts of fathers are not restored to their children, both naturally and spiritually, the second part of the scripture in Malachi 4:6 says the Lord will "strike the earth with a curse." When relationships between the generations are estranged, they become cursed.

God's heart is to take a generation that has been cursed by a breakdown of family relationships and rebuild trust. Jesus came to restore broken relationships: the relationship between God and man and the relationship between fathers and sons. This family connection was a means for blessing and restoration between the generations.

We also have to break the curse that has persisted between spiritual fathers and their estranged spiritual children. Church leaders have often been so busy with their programs and committees that they have no time to train spiritual children to become future spiritual parents themselves. This is a blight on the church, stunting future generations of leaders.

God is calling us to become spiritual parents to prepare the next generation for spiritual parenthood so He can restore a sense of responsibility of spiritual fathers and mothers toward their children.

The promise to connect fathers to children

Our God wants to convict fathers, who were once irresponsible and caught up in their own agendas, of their neglect. He alone is the one who can repair the damage and reconnect dads and moms to their lonely children. The Lord wants to restore relationships between the young and the old so that a powerful spiritual legacy can persevere and proliferate. He wants to provide relationships where spiritual fathers and mothers contribute a sense of protection to their spiritual children so that they can mature in their Christian lives.

As parents, we want to give our children a sense of protection from the madness around them. We want them to know that however terrible the world becomes, they can find comfort and shelter in a God who cares deeply about families. He has revealed Himself as our Father, and He is calling spiritual fathers to stand up and follow His example.

There are countless examples and models of spiritual parenting in the scriptures. Jesus modeled spiritual fatherhood to His twelve disciples. Paul discipled young Timothy. Elijah became a spiritual parent to Elisha. Moses trained Joshua to take his place to lead the children of Israel into the Promised Land. These types of one-on-one mentoring relationships produced a rich legacy and impartation to future generations. We need this kind of connection and impartation.

Research shows that children learn best from observing and imitating behavior that is "modeled." A father models acceptable behavior for his children. He leads rather than drives them. Modern sheepherders often drive the flock with the help of dogs, but the shepherd of ancient Israel walked ahead, and the sheep followed him. God has revealed Himself to us as a Father and He is calling fathers to follow His example. Spiritual parents are expected to model Christ-like behavior and attitudes, and their children will follow after.

Family connection in the Old and New Testaments

In the Old Testament, God's people consisted of twelve tribes and a multitude of clans and families, known corporately as the children of Israel. Through this family connection, God displayed the importance of generational inheritance which is passed from father to son. Receiving this inheritance depended on the flow of blessing from generation to generation.

The Lord continued to see His church in the New Testament as composed of believers in spiritual families. The early church knew the importance of the family connection. The scriptures tell us that God's people gathered at the temple and met in small groups in homes to minister to each other. "So continuing daily with one accord in the temple, and breaking bread from house to house, they ate their food with gladness and simplicity of heart, praising God and having favor with all the people. And the Lord added to the church daily those who were being saved" (Acts 2:46-47).

The early church modeled spiritual parenting by not only meeting in the temple, but also "house to house" so they could experience spiritual family life to its fullest. The assemblies were vibrant and alive. The believers had a deep love for each other. Joyfulness and generosity were the outstanding characteristics of these early believers. They sold their possessions to provide for the needs of others. They remained steadfast in the apostle's teachings, learned to pray with results, rejoiced when persecuted, and were willing to die for their faith. They were held in high honor by others who observed their life-style.

Relationships are the key

Relationships were the key to the kingdom of God in the early church. In these house fellowship groups, spiritual families were raised.

Through small groups meeting in homes, the members were nurtured, equipped to serve, and could easily use their spiritual gifts to build each other up to become like Christ. They met together with joy and love for each other, and new people were continually added to the church family. Who wouldn't want this?

This kind of New Testament church life, where people were in relationship with each other and their God, is a model we need to imitate. Healthy families have parents who take their God-given responsibility as fathers and mothers to their children very seriously. John, the apostle, challenges the early believers to: "practice loving each other, for love comes from God and those who are loving and kind show that they are children of God, and they are getting to know him better" (I John 4:7 TLB). Living in close relationships with others reflects that we understand and appreciate the importance of New Testament living.

A modern-day phenomenon

An amazing thing is happening across the earth today. Hundreds of thousands of small "cell groups" of believers are forming all across the globe. God's people from nearly every denomination and movement are again returning to the reality of New Testament church life as they meet from house to house during the week for prayer, fellowship, to pray for the lost, to support one another, and to experience true spiritual family relationships. And amazingly enough, this small group phenomenon is springing up in all types of churches in nearly every nation of the world. As people tire of traditional church programs, God is calling His church back to the simplicity of spiritual family life.

Last year I met Sam, an airline pilot, and his wife Janice in a city in the Pacific Northwest. Sam grew up with a religious background but had been turned off by the church. When his neighbor, Duane, invited him to attend their small group meeting in their home, Sam at first declined the invitation. He wanted nothing to do with Christianity. The Christians he knew were hypocrites and self-righteous. The Christianity he saw was all rules and regulations.

But Duane and the guys from the group persisted in reaching out to Sam. When they saw he was adding a room to his house, they offered to help. Sometime during hammering nails and laying down carpeting, Sam's perception of Christians started to change for the better.

These guys were real. They didn't spout a lot of overdone Christian cliches. They admitted their weaknesses and clearly "walked their talk." Eventually, Sam and Janice both gave their lives to the Lord. The men and women in the small group next door became their spiritual parents. As Sam gave up his bad habits one at a time, the men never condemned him, but supported him as a family should. Today, Sam and Janice lead their own small group of believers. They are now spiritual parents to others.

Built together as "living stones"

The church of Jesus Christ is built through relationships. I Peter 2:5 says we are living building-stones for God's use in building His house: "You also, as living stones, are being built up a spiritual house...." We, as redeemed people in whom God now resides, are "living stones." We are being built together in relationship into a spiritual house. We are meant to be held together by these God-ordained relationships. Without them, we soon fall apart and lay as useless rubble on the ground.

Sadly, today there are many living stones lying useless on a pile. Many Christians, instead of being vibrantly attached to other believers in God-ordained family-type relationships, are haphazardly thrown on a heap as they assemble once a week to hear a sermon and sing some songs and then leave without any real interaction. Instead of being the family God has called them to be, they come together every Sunday morning in a large non-relational gathering. Rather than experiencing a true spiritual *family,* they only experience a weekly *reunion.*

Family life or weekly reunion?

There's a huge difference between vibrant family life and an extended family getting together for a reunion. When family comes together for a *reunion,* they present their best side to the larger family. They swap stories and testimonies of their family's accomplishments and celebrate its success. They tell about the fantastic goal Jeremy made on the soccer team and that Meagan is an honor student. But much of this is superficial.

Real family know the struggles because they are there day after day. They know that Jeremy worked long and hard to reach his present caliber of soccer play and had a major setback when he broke his leg. They know Meagan had to overcome a learning disability, and it took diligent study to attain the distinction of becoming an honor student. Real family knows each other inside out. They see the good, the bad, and the ugly, and they still love each other and work as a unit to encourage each member. We can be ourselves in a family. There is no test to pass; we are included simply because we are *family*. In a spiritual family the struggles and realities are readily shared in transparent relationships—a small group interaction—with spiritual parents to guide us.

So how large should these spiritual families be? My wife LaVerne's mother came from a family of nineteen children. My father came from a family of fourteen children. LaVerne and I have only four children. There is no set rule, but true spiritual family life can best be experienced within the context of a small group of people. Jesus had twelve disciples. Moses took the advice of his father-in-law and divided the children of Israel into groups of ten. I believe that ten to twelve adults is often the limit for a spiritual family to be most effective. After there are more than twelve in a small group, it is easy to slip into the mode of having a nice meeting or reunion without experiencing the reality and blessing of honest, open relationships.

Discover family in connected relationships

Regardless of the size, it is essential for God's family to be authentic. God's family needs to be involved with each other in the nitty-gritty of life, building one another up. Trust is built through this involvement, and as a result spiritual fathering and mothering can be released.

With a growing dissatisfaction of simply attending church meetings and activities, people are looking for genuine relationships. They are looking for family-type relationships—where there is no need to impress or adopt "better-than-thou" attitudes. They want to be a part of a family where there is no superficiality. They are weary of systems that become stagnant and are simply not working.

The Lord rebukes His children in Jeremiah 2:13 for abandoning Him, the Fountain of Life-giving Water, and building faulty cisterns which the water leaked through! A cistern was used for storing rainwater and so the quantity was limited. Often the water became stale or stagnant or leaked away.

Many church systems today are stagnant and limited. A pastor is paid to do the work of ministry; the people get their money's worth—good sermons and great programs. Too often, the pastor gets bored, burns out, or moves to another church, and the people never obtain the opportunity to fulfill their calling in Christ to become equipped, empowered by His Spirit, and released as ministers themselves. They never get the chance to become fathers. We must change our focus from programs and a spectator mentality to empowering and fathering people in spiritual family settings.

Turn loose the fathers and mothers in the Lord!

If we don't change our focus, the church will continue to overflow with "emotional and spiritual orphans," according to Floyd McClung in his book *The Father Heart of God*:

> So many people are orphaned, not just from their physical parents, but from any kind of healthy spiritual or emotional heritage. The church is also filled with spiritual orphans. Either they have accepted Jesus Christ but have not been nurtured in their faith, or because of some failure on their own or someone else's part they have not yet become a part of a spiritual family. These people desperately need pastoral care. They need to be taught God's Word, to be counseled with sound biblical principles, and to be encouraged and exhorted by someone mature in the faith. They need a spiritual father or mother who can help them grow in the Lord.
>
> Others need to be "reparented"—that is, given the kind of example that only a wise, stable mother or father figure can provide. If proper parenting was missing during a person's developmental years, whether physically or spiritually or both, he or she needs someone to provide an example.
>
> Being a father or mother in the Lord is not limited to those who are pastors or spiritual leaders. There is also a very crucial need for other spiritually mature, caring people to act as "fathers" and "mothers" to other believers.
>
> By their very presence, they minister to those around them because of their maturity and depth in God. We need to turn loose these "moms and dads" in the church to be who they are. By being available, having time for people, and having an open home, their lives can be instruments of healing and love.[6]

The God of families wants us to be strengthened and rooted and grounded in love. He wants His family (the body of Christ) to connect together in the intimate ways in which a family interacts. We need the connection and individual care in the form of fathering/mothering mentoring relationships, or we will be left as spiritual orphans.

Just as natural families spend time with both their immediate family members and also extended family, the New Testament church met both in the temple and from house to house (Acts 20:20). As the church meets both in the more intimate small group settings (sometimes called *cell groups*) and larger "reunion" settings of celebrations or Sunday morning services, the pattern of reunions and small spiritual families sets the stage for the development of spiritual parenting relationships.

In the next chapter, we will discover how spiritual children grow and develop from babies, into young men (women), and finally, fathers (mothers) themselves.

Notes

[1] Robin McMillan, "In a Father's Absence," *The Morning Star Journal*, (Vol. 9 No. 4).

[2] Robert Stearns, *Prepare the Way*, (Lake Mary, Florida: Creation House, 1999), p. 101-102.

[3] Dr. David Cannistraci, *The Gift of Apostle*, (Ventura, California: Regal Books, 1996), p. 116-117.

[4] Joseph P. Shapiro, Joanne M. Schrof, "Honor Thy Children," *U.S. News & World Report*, (February 27, 1995).

[5] Ken R. Canfield, "Safe in a Father's Love," *Charisma*, June 1991.

[6] Floyd McClung, *The Father Heart of God*, (Eugene, Oregon: Harvest House Publishers, 1985), pp. 127-129.

CHAPTER 3

It's Time to Grow Up

How spiritual children become parents

According to the Bible, we go through life in stages—as little children, young men, and fathers. At each point in our journey, we function in a particular way and have distinct tasks to perform. John addresses all three spiritual stages in I John 2:12-14:

> I write to you, little children, because your sins are forgiven you for His name's sake. I write to you, fathers, because you have known Him who is from the beginning. I write to you, young men, because you have overcome the wicked one. I write to you, little children, because you have known the Father. I have written to you, fathers, because you have known Him who is from the beginning. I have written to you, young men, because you are strong, and the word of God abides in you, and you have overcome the wicked one.

Coming to a place of fatherhood is the cry of God's heart. International speaker, teacher and spiritual father, Alan Vincent from San Antonio, Texas, has this to say about these verses in I John: "The cry of the apostle John was not only for strong men who knew the Word of God and could overcome the evil one, but for *fathers* who really knew God and who would come forth to father the church. If men as a whole became strong fathers according to the biblical pattern—in home, church, and society—then most of our social problems would disappear and Satan's kingdom would be severely curtailed. Fatherhood is the foundation on which God has chosen to build the whole structure of society."

Since fatherhood is so crucial to God's divine order, He established a natural training ground consisting of "growth stages." We grow to fatherhood as we progress through each of these stages. Only then do we receive the heart and revelation of a father.

Our stages as babies in Christ, young men and women, and spiritual fathers and mothers have nothing to do with our chronological age but everything to do with how we eventually progress on to spiritual maturity. Children are expected to grow up. Only then can they become fathers and mothers.

If we fail to take the next steps to become spiritual parents, we remain spiritual babies—spiritually immature and lacking parenting skills. It is sad, but it is this scenario which is often the very case in the church. Many times there is no provision for believers to develop within our church systems. Sometimes people simply do not want to take the responsibility to parent.

Nevertheless, with the restoration of New Testament Christianity, as people meet together in small groups, God is providing an ideal setting to develop spiritual parents. Each person is given the opportunity to "do the work of ministry" and connect in vital relationships with each other. Through modeling and impartation, spiritual reproduction happens naturally.

Reproduced in a small group setting

Yasuko came as a Japanese exchange student to attend a university near Harrisburg, Pennsylvania. Her host family, who served in a cell group in our church, accepted her as one of the family and included her in all family activities, including a cell group that met in their community. Although her Buddhist parents had warned her to remain true to her Buddhist upbringing, Yasuko was overwhelmed by the love and acceptance showered on her by these Christians.

Just two days before Christmas, her host family found her crying. When asked why she was crying, she explained, "I am so happy. I am going to give you a Christmas gift," said Yasuko. "I want to tell you that today I gave my life to Jesus!" Her host family and cell group rejoiced! For the remaining few months she had in America, they discipled her and became spiritual parents to this young believer.

Yasuko returned to her homeland and is now on fire for Jesus! Today she serves as a youth pastor in Japan. She is a spiritual mother to others as she continues to receive spiritual parenting from her spiritual mom and dad in Pennsylvania, via email!

God's intention is to bring believers to the place of spiritual fatherhood, after going through spiritual childhood and young adulthood. Paul, the apostle, made it his concern to properly instruct everyone so they could be grounded in the faith: "...teaching every man in all wisdom, that we may present every man perfect in Christ Jesus" (Colossians 1:28).

The Lord's call has not changed. Like Paul, eventually everyone, after being equipped, can become a spiritual parent. Meanwhile, we have to progress through the stages of growth. Let's look at each of these stages and use them as gauges as to where we are in our spiritual maturity and how we can get to the place of becoming spiritual fathers and mothers ourselves.

Spiritual children

Natural babies are wonderful! They bring new life to a family. Parents don't mind when babies mess in their diapers because that's what babies do. Although their fussing and crying may interfere with parents' schedules, dad and mom are happy to take care of their child because he is little and defenseless and needs help. Caring parents would never deny a child their attention. Children are self-centered: they do not know any better, yet we gladly supply their needs. Babies are quick to laugh and cry, expressing their needs immediately and freely. They express simple feelings and thoughts and opinions, and we love them for it.

Spiritual babies in the body of Christ are wonderful, too! According to I John 2:12, they are children whose sins are forgiven. This forgiveness of sin puts them in fellowship with God and other believers. Spiritual children are alive to what they can receive from their Savior. They freely ask the Father when they have a need. Did you ever notice how new believers can pray prayers that seem to be theologically unsound, yet God answers almost every prayer a new believer prays? The Father is quick to take care of these little ones.

A new believer's focus is forgiveness of sins, getting to heaven and getting to know the Father. Like natural babies, they know their

Father, although it is not necessarily a thorough knowledge of God. A new believer will often act like a natural child with the marks of immaturity, including instability and gullibility. They will need constant assurance and care. They often do the unexpected because they are still learning what it means to follow Jesus. Spiritual parents are happy to spend extra time with spiritual children in order to guide them in the right direction.

Like natural babies, spiritual babies may be self-centered, selfish and irresponsible. But spiritual parents know that eventually, they will grow up. In time, they will follow a mature pattern of living as they grow into a loving relationship with Jesus Christ. Spiritual parents expect them to learn the early lessons of Christian faith and move on to new horizons. A growing person is one who constantly reaches out for maturity in personhood and personality.

But what happens when spiritual babies do not grow up? When men and women still have childish emotions, toddler angers and adolescent behaviors well into their adult years, psychologists call it "arrested development." They have simply stopped growing emotionally and are stuck in an immature stage in life. This dimension of childishness quickly loses its appeal if it does not pass with time. A childish adult is not attractive. Neither is a believer who has not grown up spiritually.

In other words, not only new believers are spiritual babies in the church today. Older Christians who lack spiritual maturity are "adults in age" but "babies in spiritual growth." They may be 20, 30, 40 or 50 years of age, Christian believers for years, and have never spiritually matured. They live self-centered life-styles, complaining and fussing and throwing temper-tantrums when things do not go their way. Some do not accept the fact that God loves them for who they are. Others may wallow in self-pity when they fail. Still others may live under an immense cloud of guilt and condemnation.

A pastor friend of mine lamented, "I have, at times, felt like I needed to walk down the aisles of our church building each Sunday to give everyone their spiritual bottles. And what really bothered me, was I felt I had to part the whiskers of some of the spiritual babies in our church to give them their spiritual bottles!"

Spiritual babies need to be spoon-fed but young men and women have learned to feed themselves as they meditate on the Word of God daily. It is time to grow up! Many spiritual children in our churches today desperately need to grow up and become spiritual young men and women and eventually become spiritual parents themselves.

Spiritual young men and women

The enthusiasm and idealism of youth is a potent force. Young adults are often able to see the simple truth of a complicated matter and are able to work tirelessly for a good cause. Fearless and strong, they bring zeal to the body of Christ. Spiritual young men and women no longer have to be spoon-fed. According to I John 2:14, the Word of God abides in them and they have learned to feed on the Word to overcome the wicked one.

When they are confused, they do not wallow in indecision but speak the Word of God to their existence. "For God is not the author of confusion but of peace..." they say, quoting I Corinthians 14:33, and trust that God will intervene for them.

They don't need to run to others in the church to care for them like babies because they have learned how to apply the Word to their own lives. When the devil tempts them, they know what to do to overcome him. They use the Word of God effectively and powerfully!

Paul gives this advice to Timothy, his young friend and spiritual son: "Don't let anyone look down on you because you are young, but set an example for the believers in speech, in life, in love, in faith and in purity" (I Timothy 4:12 NIV). We need to do everything we can to encourage those who are young. We need to allow them to begin to develop their ministries while they are young. They are strong in the Word and Spirit. They have learned to use the strength of spiritual discipline, of prayer and the study of the Word. They are alive to what they can do for Jesus—how they are strong and able to defeat the enemy.

On the other hand, the temptations of youth may be a trap for those who have not yet developed a strong sense of right and wrong. II Timothy 2:22 tells young people to: "Run from anything that gives you the evil thoughts that young men often have..." (TLB). Youth are cautioned to run from their youthful passions that might lead to scandal.

A young man or woman may have attained a certain level of spiritual maturity, but they are not yet spiritual parents. They sometimes can become arrogant and dogmatic. After returning from the latest seminar or after reading a recent book, they sometimes think they have all of the answers. They need to be tempered by parenthood. They need to become fathers and mothers to experience its joys and disciplines.

When I was eight years old, I thought my daddy knew everything. When I turned thirteen, I thought, "There are a couple of things this man doesn't know!" When I got to sixteen years of age, there were times I thought, "My father is prehistoric!" Then in my early twenties I got married, and a few years later we had our first child. I was shocked at what my father had learned in the last couple of years! You know what happened—*I* was the one who had changed! I had matured and realized my dad knew much more than I thought he did when I was sixteen. Parenthood had tempered me. Today I find my father to be one of the wisest men I know.

Spiritual fathers and mothers

Just how do spiritual young men and women grow up to become spiritual fathers and mothers? There is only one way—to have children! You could memorize the entire book of Leviticus and repeat it backwards but your knowledge and expertise would not make you a spiritual father. Spiritual parents become parents by having spiritual children; it is as simple as that!

You can become a spiritual parent either by adoption (fathering someone who is already a believer but needs to be mentored) or by natural birth (fathering someone you have personally led to Christ).

Onesimus was a natural spiritual son to Paul while Timothy was a spiritual son to Paul by adoption. Paul led Onesimus to Christ while in prison. "I appeal to you for my son Onesimus, whom I have begotten while in my chains" (Philemon 10). Paul met Timothy while in Lystra after Timothy had come to Christ earlier due to the influence of his mother and grandmother (Acts 16:1-3). Paul treated both "adopted son Timothy" and "natural son Onesimus" like spiritual sons and was committed to helping them mature spiritually.

Spiritual fathers and mothers are mature believers who have grown and matured in their Christian walk; they are called *fathers* according to I John 2:13: "I write to you, fathers, because you have known Him who is from the beginning...." This implies a profound and thorough knowledge of Jesus through knowing His Word. It also implies a deep sense of acquaintance with Him, by having a passion for Jesus. Mature Christians are awake to their calling to be like Jesus—to be a father like God's Son. They understand what it takes to be a spiritual parent and are willing to become one.

Susan, a young mother, and new believer, joined one of her church's small groups expecting to learn biblical values and be encouraged by the time she spent with fellow Christians. But something much greater happened. Liz, an older woman in the group, asked Susan if she wanted to spend time together one-on-one for extra encouragement and accountability. Of course Susan was thrilled. She expected she would listen as Liz taught her all she needed to know about living a victorious Christian life. Liz was such a spiritual giant in Susan's eyes. Not only did she know God's Word, she was the most compassionate woman Susan had ever met!

Susan's first surprise was that Liz was so low-key when they met together. She didn't lecture her or act super-spiritual. It was soon apparent that Liz really loved her, as a mother loves her daughter. Bit by bit, Susan opened up her heart to Liz. Liz was easy to talk to because she was transparent in sharing about her own struggles in her marriage, job, and family. She taught Susan how to rely on scripture for answers and prayed with her about everything.

Liz generously and selflessly poured out her life, and Susan blossomed spiritually. A new Christian was brought to maturity because she had a Christ-like role model. It happened easily and naturally within a family-type setting of a small group (spiritual family) where she experienced the love and patience of a spiritual parent. Now Susan has taken the step to become a spiritual parent herself, as she has seen by Liz' modeling.

Again, becoming a spiritual parent has nothing to do with chronological age. After working with a team to plant a new church in 1980, within the first few years it became evident that the youth of our church had a call from God to spiritual parenting. Brian Sauder, a young adult, who then served as our youth pastor, very wisely began to train key youth leaders to become spiritual parents and lead youth cell groups. When our daughter Katrina was fifteen, she served as an assistant cell leader. It was amazing to see her grow spiritually during this season of her life as she experienced becoming a spiritual parent to younger teens in her cell group.

You are eventually called to be a father

Parents today know it is not easy to raise children. Primed by racks of bestselling child-care manuals, parents are still uneasy. Just as many natural parents are unsure of their parenting skills, many potential spiritual parents feel the same. They simply do not feel ready!

I will never forget the experience of being a father for the first time. LaVerne, and I had never been down that road before. I faithfully attended prenatal classes where I learned how to coach. After about three sessions, the nurse told us she would see us at the hospital. It was scary. When the contractions started, reality hit me, and I hit the panic button.

We were going to have a baby! (Well, okay, LaVerne was, but I was on the team.) I wasn't ready! I was too young! I wasn't experienced! I wanted to tell LaVerne, "Couldn't you just put it on hold for a few months until we are ready for this?" That was not an option. It was time, and she gave birth to a beautiful baby girl. And somehow, by the grace of God, we learned that becoming new parents was not so bad. Our parents and friends were available for advice, and amazingly enough, the baby did not break!

One of the greatest catalysts to maturity as a Christian is to become a spiritual parent. Even if prospective spiritual parents do not feel ready to become parents, as they take a step of faith, and draw on the help and advice of their own spiritual mom and dad, they will find great success and fulfillment. It challenges and even changes our perspectives. We overcome spiritual pride and are stretched in all directions of growth. This is how the Lord planned it, so we can grow in maturity in Christ.

Parenting is God's idea

I was captivated by author Henri J. M. Nouwen's description of his journey to spiritual fatherhood in his book *The Return of the Prodigal Son*. In it, he tells of his fascination with Rembrandt's painting of the prodigal son in his father's arms as the elder son looks on. "Am I the elder son or the prodigal in that picture?" he agonized over the years as he searched for spiritual fulfillment. One day, a friend looked at him and spoke some powerful words:

"Whether you are the younger son or the elder son, you have to realize that you are called to become the father. You have been looking for friends all your life; you have been craving for affection as long as I've known you; you have been interested in thousands of things; you have been begging for attention, appreciation, and affirmation left and right. The time has come to claim your true vocation—to be a father who can welcome his children home without asking them any questions and without wanting anything from them in return." [1]

Like the father of the prodigal son, a spiritual father gives himself joyfully to his son because he loves him. Equipped with this affirmation and love, a son can claim his sonship and grow up and become a healthy father himself.

Are you a spiritual baby, a spiritual young man or woman, or a spiritual father or mother? God's call on all our lives is for us to eventually become spiritual parents. There will be no greater joy than to see our spiritual children walking in truth (II John 4).

What will a spiritual father really look like? In the chapter that follows, we are going to take a snapshot of a loving, spiritual father and learn what it takes to be one.

Notes
[1] Henri J.M. Nouwen, *The Return of the Prodigal Son*, (Broadway, New York: Doubleday, 1992), p. 22.

CHAPTER 4

Understanding What It Takes to Be a Father

What does a spiritual parent look like?

More than twenty-five years ago, as young youth workers, LaVerne and I began to develop what we called *Paul-Timothy discipling relationships* with new Christians. I met with a few young men each week for Bible study and prayer and LaVerne did the same with young women. Early on, we realized these relationships were going to be a work in progress, and it might be a long haul before we saw spectacular results. Many of the kids came from one particular neighborhood where motorcycle gangs and drugs were commonplace. Since most of the kids were first generation believers, they received little support from friends and family.

We were young ourselves, didn't know much, and made mistakes, but our hearts were at the right place. We knew that in order for these kids to grow spiritually and not fall away, we would have to do more than spend time in a discipleship-type Bible study with them. They needed to see Christianity practically modeled and working or none of it would make any sense to them. We didn't call it mentoring or spiritual fathering at the time, but we were doing it just the same. It was more than a duty or event for us, it was a life-style of being connected in relationships to younger Christians who desperately needed supportive, nurturing commitment from older Christians.

We opened our hearts and home to these kids and loved them unconditionally. Deep down we realized that, (although in all honesty we didn't consciously see that far ahead at the time) if we coached them to grow up spiritually, they could someday help others and it would all be worth it. So we welcomed these teenagers into our daily lives. They spent a lot of time hanging out at our house, creating permanent red Kool-aid stains on the carpet and punching occasional holes in the wall during wrestling matches.

Most of the training took place as they observed us discipling our children or fixing that persistent roof leak. We were learning step by step how to be effective spiritual parents, and they were learning how to bear fruit as Christians.

The Lord was faithful. Out of these inauspicious beginnings, a church was birthed with some of these young believers who were being trained to take on the next batch of spiritual children. Today, at DOVE Christian Fellowship International (DCFI) we have the privilege of watching many of our spiritual children, grandchildren, and great grandchildren reproduce spiritual sons and daughters as new cell groups and new churches are being planted throughout the world. It is so fulfilling!

There was nothing special about us and there still isn't! We were ordinary young people, made lots of mistakes, and have many stories to tell that are not success stories, but we had the heart of fathers to teach their children. We loved Jesus, we really loved those kids, and as any parent, we expected them to grow!

Fathers expect their children to grow

Parents expect their children to grow up in every way—physically, spiritually, mentally and emotionally. Through the natural progression of time and with much love and the right amount of training, children are expected to mature into healthy adults and move out to start homes of their own.

As I mentioned before, having our first child was quite an experience for me. Like myself, most parents do not feel they are ready to have children because they are inexperienced. But having a baby will change all that. Parents quickly get around the clock, hands-on-training! Just as we learn to raise our natural children, we learn to train spiritual children simply by doing it.

Twenty-one years after having our first child, I walked down the aisle with this "baby" girl at my side on her wedding day. I realized I spent all those years of time, effort and money to give her away to her fiance! We raised her to give her away. Recently she and her husband gave us our first grandson. Now they will have the opportunity to be parents and prepare the next generation. Parenting is all about passing on a legacy. Spiritual parenting involves a whole package of loving, training, modeling, imparting, and multiplying.

A spiritual father defined

Before you can ever be a spiritual father or mother, you must first check your motives. Spiritual fathering is a "behind the scenes" kind of deal. Probably no one will pat you on the back and say, "What a good job you are doing: keep up the good work." Why? Because being a father is not something you *do*, as much as it is something you *are.* I do not have to tell people that I'm a father. They know it when they see my son and daughters at my side.

Scripture warns us about giving ourselves an impressive title in an effort to try to gain the honor and respect of others: "Do not call anyone on earth your father; for One is your Father, He who is in heaven...But he who is greatest among you shall be your servant" (Matthew 23:9,11). A spiritual father is always a servant first. Paul, the apostle, called himself a father several times in scripture, but he uses the word "father" to denote, "not *authority*, but *affection*: therefore he calls them not his *obliged*, but his *beloved*, sons" (see I Corinthians 4:14).[1] The measure of greatness of a spiritual father is his level of servanthood and love.

Spiritual fathers and mothers could also be called *mentors* or *coaches* because they are in a place to help sons and daughters negotiate the obstacles of their spiritual journeys. A coach is someone who wants to see you win. A coach tells you that you can make it. Simply stated, my favorite definition of a spiritual father would be: *A spiritual father helps a spiritual son reach his God-given potential.* It is that uncomplicated and yet profound. Bobb Biehl says it this way: "Mentoring is more 'how can I help you?' than 'what should I teach you?'"[2]

Of course, a spiritual father *will* teach spiritual truths, but his energies go into *caring for and helping* the son in all aspects of life. A spiritual fathering relationship cannot be a formal relationship of teaching because by definition and by practice, it is informal interaction. It takes place along the highways and byways of life. A spiritual son needs to see his father in action in everyday life. A spiritual father loves and gently encourages his son to move in the right direction as he progresses on his journey.

Paul, the apostle, showed how much he loved the Thessalonian believers as a spiritual parent in his letter to them: "But we were gentle among you, just as a nursing mother cherishes her own children. So, affectionately longing for you, we were well pleased to impart to you not only the gospel of God, but also our own lives, because you had become dear to us" (I Thessalonians 2:7-8).

Paul cherished the people he had mentored like a nursing mother, tender and gentle. When spiritual children are impacted with a father's and mother's affection, they know it and respond to this love. They know when they are genuinely loved and accepted!

With a mature spiritual father at his side, a son will grow strong and learn quickly and naturally by example. He teaches, trains, sets a good example, and provides a role model. A spiritual father raises a son's awareness of attitudes or behaviors in his life that need to be changed. He helps him take an honest look at his life and make adjustments so that his actions and behavior can change.

Similarities between a spiritual and natural father

Spiritual fathering needs to be taught and imparted just as natural fathering is imparted. "There are at least five similarities between a spiritual father and a natural father which help to open our eyes to the function of a New Testament spiritual father," according to Dr. David Cannistraci. If we understand these functions, it will not only help us to prepare the way for spiritual fathers, but will also assist us in recognizing them as they appear:

1. Fathers demonstrate love. The love relationship between a father and his son provides the ideal environment for training and developing the character and life of the son. Without love, a son may grow, but he cannot flourish...Fathers affirm their children and provide the gentle security of an unwavering commitment to their well-being.

2. Fathers train and discipline. Fathers take a powerful part in firmly directing and guiding their children into activities and attitudes that will prepare them for success. A true father accepts responsibility for his children. The biblical role of a father is to raise his children to a place of maturity and fruitfulness.

3. Fathers provide. Another primary task of a father is to provide for his children. To "provide" means to sustain and enrich....What does a spiritual father provide for his spiritual children? A legacy of spirit can only come from a spiritual father to his spiritual children.

4. Fathers reproduce. In the most basic sense, natural fathers are men who have physically contributed to creating a new life...Spiritual fathers give spiritual life to new children in the faith by becoming the vessels through which those children enter into the new birth. They continue their ministries as fathers by raising up and reproducing their own ministries within such lives.

5. Fathers bless and impart. Many fathers understand well how to love, provide for and train their children, but many lack the ability the great apostolic fathers of the early church profitably exercised—imparting spiritual blessing. The apostle Paul pictures God the Father blessing us as His children with all spiritual blessings through our relationship with Christ (Ephesians 1:3). The apostle Paul laid his hands on his spiritual son Timothy and was used to impart gifts and blessings that Timothy was responsible to utilize (II Timothy 1:6). This transference of divine life is one of the most awesome responsibilities of a spiritual father. Speaking from experience, I can say that this is one of the greatest experiences any spiritual son can have.[3]

Fathers have "been with Jesus"

A spiritual father does not have to be a spiritual giant in order to train others. No one is a finished product. We are all learning to live in obedience to God and growing in amazing grace. What really counts is our hearts and Who resides there. The important thing is that we "have been with Jesus."

Peter and John had no formal education, but they spoke fluently to the scholarly religious leaders of the Sanhedrin: "Now when they saw the boldness of Peter and John, and perceived that they were uneducated and untrained men, they marveled. And they realized that they had been with Jesus" (Acts 4:13).

God will take common, ordinary people who love Jesus and transform them. Spiritual growth is recognizing who it is that God calls us to be and overcoming adversity through the power of the Holy Spirit. God will use us at any point in our Christian walk if we allow Him to.

Fathers are models

By His example, Jesus modeled spiritual fathering. Though He ministered to the multitudes, He spent most of His time on earth as a spiritual father to twelve men. He knew that kingdom values were caught more than taught. He trained them so they could grow up spiritually and be equipped to train others. He fished, prayed, wept and rejoiced with these disciples, and they went on to "father" many more people in the kingdom of God.

When Jesus trained His disciples, He didn't tell them how to be disciples by having them sit on a hill somewhere and lecturing them for three years. He taught them from real life experiences as they traveled from place to place and actively learned, by Jesus' example and demonstration, about the kingdom of God. The disciples witnessed firsthand God's power and compassion when they came to Jesus for bread to feed a hungry multitude. They learned to discern the true from the false when Jesus exposed the scribes and Pharisees in their false piety and self-righteousness.

Jesus was totally accessible and approachable to His disciples for three years, and they grew spiritually mature with His tutelage. They were not perfect, but He believed in them enough to entrust the church to them when He ascended into heaven.

In the book of Colossians, Paul, the apostle, modeled fatherhood to Epaphras when he made himself available in a time of need. It seems that Epaphras had been converted and carried the gospel to Colossae. Because of his previous relationship to Paul, Epaphras felt at liberty to come to Rome to seek Paul's seasoned counsel on the errors then threatening the Colossian church. In response, Paul wrote this letter to the church as a father who cared deeply because he felt a stewardship for the people through his relationship with Epaphras (Colossians 1:25). Fathers who model fatherhood like this perpetuate a legacy through their sons as the sons learn how to father others into the kingdom.

Fathers set an example

In order to grow in God, people need someone to speak into their lives. Paul spoke into the lives of those he fathered in the faith: "Remember those who rule over you, who have spoken the word of God to you, whose faith follow..." (Hebrews 13:7). Paul presented a true and godly example to those he served, and they would gladly imitate him. This initiated a legacy of spiritual parenting.

In I Thessalonians 2:11, Paul reminds the church that he set the example as a father, exhorting, comforting and charging each believer: "as a father does his own children." Providing an example for others to imitate and reproduce is an important aspect of spiritual parenting.

Fathers give sons a sense of significance

One goal of a father is to strive to build a healthy sense of self-worth in his son. In his book, *Seven Things Children Need*, John Drescher says every child wants to be noticed and recognized as a person of worth. "It is almost impossible to live with ourselves if we feel we are of little value or if we don't like ourselves," he says. "A person who feels like a nobody will contribute little to life. This needs to be stressed because the great plague of inferiority feelings starts early in life. We human beings need to be noticed, appreciated, and loved as we are if we are to have a sense of significance." [4]

A few months ago, Bert Rosman, a young Dutch church planter in Croatia told me how grateful he is for the spiritual fathers and mothers who believe in him and his wife, greatly impacting their lives on the mission field. "Spiritual fathers give us identity, security, self-esteem, value and destiny," he asserted.

Leaders often become leaders only when someone believes in them as leaders. Years ago, there was a young believer in our cell group who felt like he could not pray in public. He admitted he felt inadequate among all the more mature Christians whose prayers came easily. I did not give Keith a formula to follow, but I saw potential in him and encouraged him to step out of his "comfort zone."

One day, he urged me, "Ask me to pray sometime when I'm not expecting it." I was happy to oblige! Very soon, at a small group meeting, I asked Keith to begin our prayer session with a one sentence prayer. It was a place to start, and Keith prayed because I believed he could do it. My trust in him helped him to overcome his feelings of inadequacy. He went on to assume leadership in a small group and later served as a deacon in his local church.

Spiritual children will grow in responsibility and achievement when someone believes in them. Parents must see their children in the light of who they can become.

Fathers see the potential

Recognizing the undeveloped traits of a son or daughter is a father and mother's responsibility. Jesus changed Simon's name to Peter, meaning *rock*. Peter didn't act like a solid, stable rock when he fell asleep in the Garden or denied Jesus three times, but Jesus knew Peter's heart. Peter later became the *rock* Jesus predicted he would be.

Although spiritual parents cannot predict their son's or daughter's future, they can help them to set goals and to use and develop their gifts now so that God will be able to use them to serve Him and others more fully in the future.

It should also be noted that Jesus did not nag Peter to grow up after He called him a rock. Ephesians 6:4 includes advice to fathers to train their children (see their potential) and not unduly criticize them: "And you, fathers, do not provoke your children to wrath, but bring them up in the training and admonition of the Lord." Children will not reach their potential if parents exasperate them with unrealistic expectations or constant criticisms.

A spiritual father should not be too quick to correct his son's mistakes, or expect too much too soon. Although honesty is important and we cannot overlook a fault if it hinders our son's walk with the Lord, we should be slow to barge in and correct him. Sometimes a father will see a weakness but realize the best way for his son to overcome the weakness is for the son to discover it himself. The father simply makes sure he is available to help process the weakness when it surfaces. Instead of pointing out the fault too quickly, we should pray for them and stimulate them with our encouraging words. Remember, it is the Holy Spirit who leads us into all truth (John 16:13).

Fathers are available

A spiritual father or mother is an unselfish individual. They will make themselves accessible and available. Today's society, especially in the Western world, encourages us to be individualistic and selfish with our time. We fill our calendars to the maximum with work-related tasks, but make sure we pencil in generous time slots for recreation and taking care of "Number One."

A spiritual fathering relationship is marked by its liberality. Spiritual fathers give of their time generously and sacrificially. With an open heart and hand they purposefully take their spiritual children under their wings. It is not always comfortable to make ourselves available at 2 AM in the morning for a crisis phone call, but a spiritual father will graciously take it in stride because he loves his son.

According to John Drescher, our children need our time. He encourages parents to take time "to listen to [a child's] concerns, drop the newspaper when he speaks, look into his eyes when he talks to us." He tells this story of a son needing the attention of his father:

A small boy watched his father polish the car. He asked, "Dad, your car's worth a lot, isn't it?"

"Yes," his dad replied, "it cost a lot. It pays to take care of it. When I trade the car in, it will be worth more if I take care of it."

After some silence the son said, "Dad, I guess I'm not worth very much, am I?" [5]

When spiritual fathers spend time with their sons, their sons know they are worth a great deal in the fathers' eyes. A father knows that when he invests his life in nurturing his son, the son will grow up to be spiritually productive.

Fathers impart

A father will experience the joys of fathering when he takes what he has and imparts it to others. *To impart* means *to give to another what one is/has.* Through a spiritual father's teaching and influence, an impartation is conferred to his spiritual son.

Natural parents want to see their children grow into maturity. They teach them by example because they know that if they do a good job, their lineage will be a prosperous and healthy one. The parenting process has at its core the intention of raising healthy children who can produce more productive and healthy children.

This is also the heart's cry of a spiritual father or mother. Their goal is for their children to reach their full potential as men and women of God. In a spiritual parenting relationship, all of this takes place in an atmosphere of patient love and acceptance, without judgment or fear of gossip. It is meant to happen naturally and easily by example and modeled behavior as spiritual parents impart a blessing to their spiritual children.

Start where you are

Perhaps you never had a spiritual father or mother. That does not mean you are unable to be one. If you wait until you think you are ready it will probably never happen. You don't need to be perfect, just faithful and obedient. Mother Teresa once said, "God does not demand that I be successful. God demands that I be faithful. When facing God, results are not important. Faithfulness is what is important."[6]

Perhaps you feel that you already tried and failed. A few years ago, Murray McCall, who has spent the past eight years in church planting in New Zealand, told me, "After going through a season of discouragement as a spiritual leader, I came to understand that God had called me to be a father." This truth set him free as a leader in the body of Christ. He realized his primary call was to simply be a father, and he could trust God for grace to start again when he made mistakes or was discouraged.

The Bible is filled with examples and models for us to imitate— the impartation from Moses to Joshua; Elijah to Elisha; Samuel to David; Paul to Timothy and Titus. We should expect every Christian to become a spiritual father or mother as they impart to others what God has given to them. It is possible and achievable!

By way of summary and description of a spiritual father, I love this real life example of Dan Hitzhusen, a church planter, who describes his mentoring relationship with Josh McDowell:

> Josh saw me as a diamond in the rough. I was twenty-one years old with a heart for God, full of life, and full of myself. Serving as a personal assistant to Josh McDowell as a staff member of Campus Crusade for Christ, I made many mistakes. Josh expected excellence, yet, when I blew it, he would say something like, "Dan, that just shows it can happen to the best of them."

I remember really messing something up and asking Josh why he didn't get particularly angry with me. He said, "Dan, the things that I think will make you a better person, a better friend, a better representative of Jesus Christ, I share with you. Everything else I take to God." On another occasion, I was feeling rejected by some of my co-workers. Josh pulled me aside and said, "Dan, you and I are renegades. We are different. We will never really fit in. You will never fit in. That isn't the way God made you." Josh always believed in me more than I believed in myself. Perhaps the greatest personal tribute that I have for Josh McDowell is that he saw me for who God made me to be and he encouraged me to serve God with my whole heart in my own uniqueness."[7]

The Lord is placing a desire within mature Christians of our generation to be spiritual fathers and mothers to the next generation. Relationships between the young and the old are a key to the kingdom. The Lord wants to bring the young and the old together, bind them close to each other and to their God, and teach them to build His kingdom together. All it takes is willingness, availability, time, and a generous dose of the grace of God.

In the next chapter, we are going to examine the role women play in parenting relationships and the mother-heart of God.

Notes

[1] *Matthew Henry's Commentary in One Volume,* (Grand Rapids, Michigan: Zondervan, 1960), p. 119.

[2] Bobb Biehl, *Mentoring,* (Nashville, Tennessee: Broadman & Holman Publishers, 1996), p. 19.

[3] Dr. David Cannistraci, *The Gift of Apostle,* (Ventura, California: Regal Books, 1996), p. 120-124.

[4] John M. Drescher, *Seven Things Children Need,* (Scottdale, Pennsylvania: Herald Press, 1976), p. 19.

[5] Ibid., p. 27.

[6] *Mother Teresa In My Own Words,* Compiled by Jose Luis Gonzalez-Balado, (Random House, 1996), p. 40.

[7] Bobb Biehl, *Mentoring,* (Nashville, Tennessee: Broadman & Holman Publishers, 1996), p. 92.

CHAPTER 5

Spiritual Mothering

God's nurturing, mother's heart

There is a desperate need for spiritual mothers in the church of Jesus Christ today. Teenage girls, new mothers and pastors' wives throughout the body of Christ are crying out for spiritual mothers. Women need spiritual mothers to place their arms around them, protect and mentor them as they progress on their journey with Christ.

I have included this chapter which focuses on women and their unique approach and role in parenting because I want to look at the role of the mother-heart of God as it relates to spiritual parenting. We need to see this very important nurturing side of God

God created men and women to be unique with respect to one another. The differences between men and women are meant to be a blessing and bring balance to life so we can have a richer and fuller comprehension of the Father's love for us. One day, nine-year-old Joey got off the bus from school and said, "Mom, the bus is so empty we each could have our own seat. But those dumb girls, they all pile into one seat!"

Joey's maleness could not quite comprehend the female's need to cluster! Women seem to be programmed to need intimacy and deep friendships. Feminine traits are often described as soft, nurturing, intuitive and empathic. Women see themselves in relation to the people around them, preferring intimacy to separateness. This allows women to be uniquely in tune with close relationships.

When women get together, they often talk about their feelings and relationships, their work and their family. Women's nurturing, mothering characteristics come out as they communicate with each other.

The nurturing tendency in women is most evident by their capacity for love that often goes beyond that of men. Proverbs 10:1 states, "A wise son maketh a glad father: but a foolish son is the heaviness of his mother." A mother usually feels deeper pain because her love is more tender.

Of course, you don't have to be a biological mother to display tenderness and compassion. Any Christian woman who understands the father-heart of God and His everlasting love will develop nurturing, maternal characteristics.

The mother-heart of God

How do we know God has a tender, nurturing mother's heart? We have only to look at His name. One Hebrew name for God is *El Shaddai*. *El* comes from the root meaning *might and strength*. *Shad* is Hebrew for *breast* or *many-breasted one*. It shows tenderness and the desire to nurture us and make us fruitful.

Time and time again in the holy scriptures we get a picture of God's nurturing, mother-like tendencies: "Can a mother forget the baby at her breast and have no compassion on the child she has borne? Though she may forget, I will not forget you! See, I have engraved you on the palms of my hands..." (Isaiah 49:15-16a NIV). God's deep, abiding love for us is greater than even that strongest of bond between a baby and his mother. A little later on in Isaiah 66:13, the Lord says, "As a mother comforts her child, so will I comfort you...." (NIV).

The scriptures show another picture of God's nurturing and tender mother's heart in Matthew 23:37 when Christ shows His compassion for those who rejected Him: "O Jerusalem, Jerusalem, you who kill the prophets and stone those sent to you, how often I have longed to gather your children together, as a hen gathers her chicks under her wings, but you were not willing" (NIV).

Jerusalem was where the gospel was first preached and also where the Christians were first persecuted. Jesus longed to bestow His wonderful grace and favor to these spiritually blinded religious leaders in Jerusalem. Even though they refused His love, it was compassionately extended to them just as a mother hen gathers her chicks for protection, safety, warmth and comfort under her wings.

The Titus 2 mandate

I believe the Lord is calling spiritual mothers today to obey His call to take spiritual daughters under their wings. Christian women need spiritual mothers to help them grow into healthy women of God. A spiritual mother walks alongside another woman and puts her arm around her and says, "You can make it!" In her book *Spiritual Mothering*, Susan Hunt's definition for spiritual mothering is this: "When a woman possessing faith and spiritual maturity enters into a nurturing relationship with a younger woman in order to encourage and equip her to live for God's glory." [1]

God's Word gives women a clear mandate and model for spiritual mothering. Paul exhorted Titus what to teach, and into this context he exhorted older women to put their energies into training and teaching younger women: "[Teach] the older women...that they be reverent in behavior, not slanderers, not given to much wine, teachers of good things—that they admonish the younger women to love their husbands, to love their children, to be discreet, chaste, homemakers, good, obedient to their husbands, that the word of God may not be blasphemed" (Titus 2:2-5).

Paul knew the church could be impacted if older women would start teaching younger women by their godly life-styles. If they would give of themselves and invest their energies in younger women, the kingdom would be advanced. God wants to use women of reverence (who fear God), women who are free from slander, and women who are not captive to addictive behavior. These mature women are the kind of women who are ready to be spiritual mothers.

Spiritually mature women unselfishly give of themselves. They submit their will to God and to His leadership. Out of love for Him, they have learned the secret of Philippians 2:3-4: "Let nothing be done through selfish ambition or conceit, but in lowliness of mind let each esteem others better than himself [herself]. Let each of you look out not only for his [her] own interests, but also for the interests of others." Spiritually mature women will not be absorbed entirely by their own concerns but will unselfishly look out for others.

Our need for mothering

As a young, twenty-eight-year-old pastor's wife, LaVerne struggled in the early days of ministry because of the pressure she felt to conform to the expected pastor's wife role of organizing women's groups, meetings and programs. As she tells it, "I knew I was not going to be the typical pastor's wife who played the piano, organ or sang. I just did not feel called to occupy my time with being a public person. I knew God did not call me to spend my time heading committees and planning women's events. My heart's cry was to be a servant of the Lord Most High. Every time I got down on my knees, I knew what God had called me to do. It was clear—train a few women at a time."

So LaVerne spent the next few years doing just that. She started to pour her life into a few of the women who were small group leaders in the church. It wasn't a job for the fainthearted. The relationships she developed took time and effort. She was not standing up front to an adoring public.

For years, she simply trained women behind the scenes. She loved them as she inquired how their marriages were faring. She prayed and wept with them as they went through life's hard spots and rejoiced with them when they experienced life's joys. The results of this kind of spiritual mothering had far-reaching effects. These women were equipped to pass on to other women the impartation they had received. The results were a multiplication over and over again of LaVerne's initial efforts with a few women.

Today, LaVerne continues to mentor women one-on-one. When she speaks to larger crowds, the heart's cry of women is often one of "But where are the older women? Where is that spiritual mother who will mentor me and help me grow up in my Christian life?" With tears streaming down their faces, younger women are saying, "Sometimes I could just use an hour of a spiritually mature woman's time. I so desperately need to be encouraged to look to the Father. I need to hear from someone who has spiritual maturity beyond mine and can teach me valuable lessons from life." What women are looking for is a friend, a coach, a cheerleader who can point them to Jesus.

Our focus must be upward

It takes a special kind of grace to be a natural and spiritual mother in today's world. Being a mother is not easy. There is a huge mental investment, along with the physical exertion of the twenty-four hours a day demand that is required for motherhood. A woman who understands this is willing to admit her total dependence on the grace of the Lord for spiritual parenting.

Although it is important to have loving and nurturing one-on-one relationships, these relationships must hinge on the more important vertical relationship with God. A spiritual mother-daughter relationship needs to focus on glorifying God and yielding to His will and purpose.

A plaque in a mother's kitchen reads, "The greatest thing a mother can do for her children is to love their father." You could paraphrase that adage to say, "The greatest thing a spiritual mother can do for her spiritual children is to love her heavenly Father!" The entire focus of the relationship must be one of glorifying God.

This point is brought out clearly in Luke, chapter one, as we witness the interaction between Elizabeth and Mary. Elizabeth and Mary had a lot in common. They both had unusual pregnancies! When they first met, they could have focused on their unique situations and talked of all they were feeling, empathizing with each other and calling attention to their own needs. Instead, upon greeting each other, their focus was upward. Their relationship was not formed by what they needed from each other. Elizabeth, like a seasoned spiritual mother, encouraged Mary who, in turn, burst forth in praise to God:

> And it happened, when Elizabeth heard the greeting of Mary, that the babe leaped in her womb; and Elizabeth was filled with the Holy Spirit. Then she spoke out with a loud voice and said, "Blessed are you among women, and blessed is the fruit of your womb! But why is this granted to me, that the mother of my Lord should come to me? For indeed, as soon as the voice of your greeting sounded in my ears, the babe leaped in my womb for joy. Blessed is she who believed, for there will be a fulfillment of those things which were told her from the Lord."

> And Mary said: "My soul magnifies the Lord, and my spirit has rejoiced in God my Savior. For He has regarded the lowly state of His maidservant; For behold, henceforth all generations will call me blessed. For He who is mighty has done great things for me, and holy is His name" (Luke 1:41-49).

The purpose of a spiritual mothering relationship is to glorify God. He is your entire hope: "...Christ in you, the hope of glory" (Colossians 1:27). What an awesome concept.

Christ, the anointed One, lives within you! It is Christ who is ministering through you. It's not so much about what you do for God, but what God is doing in you! You need to allow Him to do the spiritual mothering through you as you yield to Him.

Relationship must be birthed in prayer

Spiritual mothering cannot be just another item on your "to do" list. Christian women today have enough meetings to attend and things to do. Developing a spiritual mothering relationship must be something the Lord imparts to you personally.

It needs to be birthed in prayer. Pray initially that the Lord will lead you to the right relationship. Then pray diligently every day for your spiritual daughter. "The effective, fervent prayer of a righteous man [woman] avails much" (James 5:16b).

What hinders spiritual mothering?

Remember that it is the character of Christ that qualifies an individual to be a spiritual mother. Potential spiritual mothers must be women who fear God. This means they need to care more about what God thinks of them than what other people think. Suffering from a poor self-image will hinder spiritual mothering. There are pressures in life to conform and act a certain way. But when the fear of God comes on a woman, she asks God what He thinks of her. She knows Christ accepts her because of the blood, and it is an unconditional love. This brings freedom in her life.

LaVerne was speaking at a women's retreat about God's unconditional love, and a woman who had been a Christian for a long time came up to her and said, "I don't think I understand God's unconditional love. Growing up, I felt love from my parents only when I performed satisfactorily for them. So I've always put conditions on my love when I related to others."

That day, she acknowledged her wrong thinking and chose to accept God's unfathomable, unconditional love for her. Her life was changed! God loves individuals whether they perform or not. His love is extended without conditions. When God's people understand this, they will not minister to others out of duty, but out of His love for them. It is through this love that we serve one another (Galatians 5:13). Another thing that will hinder spiritual mothering is selfishness. "I'm too busy," "I've raised my children," "I'm retired; just let me relax by the ocean," are all selfish excuses for not getting involved.

LaVerne has had several spiritual mothers, including Naomi, who, several years ago, at 48 years of age and after raising seven children of her own, took in a young foster son. Then her elderly mother moved in with her family. Some would look at her and say, "Isn't it time to take a break and ease up at your age?" But Naomi still found time to get together with LaVerne (she had to get a baby-sitter for her son and elderly mother at home) to pray with her.

"When I feel lazy and want to gripe and complain," said LaVerne, "I just can't make excuses for myself because I have a spiritual mom in my life who doesn't have it easy but she chooses to walk in joy."

Age factor

Chronological age does not dictate when someone can be a spiritual parent. You can be a spiritual parent when you are 16 or 80. At age 12, our daughter Charita became a spiritual parent to younger kids in a small group ministry. She took them under her wing and taught them simple biblical principles from God's Word. She prayed with them and cared for them when they had a need. Charita was learning by *doing*. Out of her love for Jesus and those kids, she took a step of obedience. She did not wait until she felt she was totally equipped; she became a spiritual parent to the kids while she was learning herself.

You can always find someone younger spiritually whom you can disciple and train in the ways of God, and soon they, too, will be ready to train others. We need to learn how to release spiritual parents of all ages to reproduce themselves.

When the Bible exhorts older women to train younger women, most likely it is meant that a spiritual mother should be a mature woman who reflects *experience*. This does not necessarily mean an "older in age" woman needs to mentor a "younger in age" woman. *Age* has less to do with it than *experience*. Experience and spiritual maturity should be the yardstick measuring who should mentor whom. Regardless of age, it is the woman's spiritual maturity that qualifies her to mentor another.

So, technically, a woman in her twenties who is spiritually mature could be a spiritual mother to a fifty-year-old woman new to the Christian faith. Recently, I met for breakfast with a medical doctor who came to faith in Christ in his forties. He spoke endearingly of a spiritual father in his life, much younger in age, who helped him grow in his newly found faith.

This younger-in-age father and older son variance may be the exception, however. More often, I believe the biblical mandate of spiritual mothering and fathering normally follows the pattern of age. Because it is the older person with years of experience, who has been already through many different seasons in life, who can more effectively mentor a younger person. Nevertheless, in both dynamics, the age differences work together to enrich the relationship.

Where do I start?

If you feel you cannot become a spiritual mother until you have had one yourself, break out of that mind-set! Instead, take a step of faith and become a spiritual mother to another woman and see what the Lord will do. God's Word says we will reap what we sow (Galatians 6:7). Sow what you have into another's life and God will bring a spiritual mother(s) into *your* life.

Of course, there is no magic formula for developing a relationship with a spiritual daughter. You just have to go and do it. Every person is unique and will find what works in each relationship. In some cases, a younger woman will approach an older woman and ask her to pray about serving for a season as a spiritual mother. At other times, the spiritual mother may approach a potential spiritual daughter first. Only the Lord can put these relationships together. If you have tried in the past and it has not worked out, continue to pray and trust Him for His "divine connection." He is faithful.

Start by praying for the woman God is calling you to mother spiritually. Perhaps you see someone who needs encouragement. Initiate a relationship by helping in practical ways—baby-sit for a single mom so she can have a night out. Go to the grocery store for a mother with toddlers. Spend time with a single woman needing encouragement. Invite a younger woman into your home for tea. Consider writing notes or making encouraging phone calls to the woman. Get to know her and her history. Share your testimonies with each other. Spend time together in Bible study if she is a young Christian and needs to be grounded in the Word. Discover her areas of struggle and pray for her: "Confess your trespasses to one another, and pray for one another, that you may be healed" (James 5:16a). With acceptance, patience and love be willing to listen and gently counsel: "Perfume and incense bring joy to the heart, and the pleasantness of one's friend springs from his [her] earnest counsel" (Proverbs 27:9 NIV).

If you are already the woman's friend, you may feel God's tug at your heart to open your life more fully to her. Take the time to invest in the relationship and be strong on encouragement! As you develop your mentoring relationship, you will experience the closeness of true friendship.

Share your uncloaked life

At the Last Supper, Jesus took off His outer garment and knelt down and washed the disciples' feet, saying, "For I have given you an example, that you should do as I have done to you" (John 13:15). Before an individual can serve others, she or he must take off their "outer garments." Although an outer garment is usually cast off when we are ready to get to some serious work, we can also look at the outer garment as a metaphor for the "Sunday best" *behavior* we must cast off. Sometimes our "outer garment behavior" is a cover-up to hide our vulnerabilities. We don't want others to see our weaknesses, so we keep our outer garments pulled around us, intact and stiff, getting in the way of real servanthood.

It can get complex and risky when we open up our lives to others. But honesty is humbling and liberating. A "performance mentality" will go out the door when we share our real, uncloaked lives with others. Uncloaked, we will no longer serve because we think it is required of us but because we love as He loved us.

Love is the key! In the next chapter, we will see how the security of our heavenly Father's love shapes us into loving spiritual mothers and fathers.

Notes
[1]   Susan Hunt, *Spiritual Mothering*, (Wheaton, Illinois: Crossway Books, 1992), p.12.

CHAPTER 6

You Can't Give What You Don't Have

Spiritual fathers and mothers must be secure in the Father's love

A s a young man, I worked on a construction crew building new houses. I learned that the first step to building a sturdy house was to put in a solid concrete foundation. It took time to level the blocks and secure them with concrete, but a solid foundation would keep the house safe when the inevitable storms and wind came. The same is true of our spiritual lives. We cannot aspire to help others and become spiritual parents without building a firm foundation on Jesus Christ. We must get to know Jesus intimately and surrender all that we are and hope to be to Him. Only then can we have something enduring to offer to others.

Millions of people today believe that God is the creator of the universe, but fewer choose to know Him deeply and experience a relationship with Him as a Father. Our Father is a God of relationship. He wants to be our Father and have a personal friendship with us so He can reveal His ways to us.

In His intercessory prayer, Jesus claims that it is possible to know the Father: "And this is eternal life, that they may know You, the only true God, and Jesus Christ whom You have sent" (John 17:3). God revealed Himself to us through Jesus Christ. The entire gospel rests on this claim that knowing God, through Jesus, brings eternal life. When we know Jesus and develop a love relationship with Him, we will be secure as believers, willing and ready to reach out to others in love. Spiritual parents know that it is only the love of the Lord that can impact a life deeply enough to create lasting change.

Secure in the Father's love

Jesus knew He was a love gift from the Father to the world. Because of this, Jesus was secure in His Father's love. Jesus knew where He came from. He knew why He was here and where He was going.

In the upper room, Jesus was so completely secure that He could serve his spiritual sons expecting nothing in return. "Jesus, knowing that the Father had given all things into His hands, and that He had come from God and was going to God, rose from supper and laid aside His garments, took a towel and girded Himself. After that, He poured water into a basin and began to wash the disciples' feet, and to wipe them with the towel with which He was girded" (John 13:3-5).

If we are to become healthy spiritual fathers and mothers, we must be certain of our Father's love for us and live in close relationship to Him. Only secure spiritual fathers, who are totally convinced that the heavenly Father loves them, can pass on a healthy spiritual inheritance to the next generation.

Why do you think Jesus' disciples turned the world upside down in a few short years? They did not change the world because they attended all the right seminars but because they lived in close, intimate relationship with the right Person! Let's look at how two of Jesus' friends, John and Mark, became fathers to the next generation of believers as they grew secure in the love of their heavenly Father.

Secure to love unconditionally

The scripture shows us that John and Jesus enjoyed an intimate, special friendship. John himself (the writer of the gospel of John) declares repeatedly that he was the disciple "whom Jesus loved." At the Passover supper, as was customary of the Greeks and Romans at mealtime, he was in a reclining position beside Jesus, "leaning on Jesus' bosom"[1] and he refers to himself as "the disciple whom Jesus loved." While standing near the cross during Jesus' crucifixion, John refers to himself as the "one whom Jesus loved."[2] At the scene of the resurrection, John again declares himself as the "one whom Jesus loved."[3] John called himself "the disciple whom Jesus loved" when he told Peter, "It is the Lord!" after Jesus' resurrection.[4] When Jesus exhorted Peter regarding how he would die, Peter asked (referring to John), "What about him?" and again John refers to himself as "the disciple Jesus loved."[5] John was totally convinced that he was accepted and loved by Jesus! He knew Jesus like a brother and was a devoted friend. It is clear that he was secure in the love of his Master. How did he get to this place in his life? It did not happen overnight. Jesus slowly nurtured change in John's life while bringing him the honor and recognition as being "the disciple Jesus loved."

Initially, before he matured, John's actions were less than desirable. He was hungry for status and power and seemed to have quite a few rough edges. John and his brother James were nicknamed "sons of thunder."[6] I picture them as tough guys, maybe the equivalent of a modern day motorcycle gang. These brothers probably had powerful and fiery temperaments. When the Samaritans refused to allow Jesus and His disciples to come through their village, they asked Jesus if they could order fire down from heaven to burn up this village of inhospitable Samaritans.[7] At this point in John's life, he certainly was not modeling the Spirit of Christ!

Another time, John and his brother earned the anger of the other disciples by asking if they could sit on Jesus' right and left hand in glory.[8] In fact, in one case, they sent their mother to implore Jesus for special favors, showing signs of insecurity and self-seeking. Another time, John saw a man driving out demons in Jesus' name, but the man was not a part of "their group."[9] In John's insecurity, he tried to stop the demon exorciser. Jesus rebuked John for his sectarian attitude.

Later, however, we see that John imparts the Holy Spirit to Philip's converts in Samaria, the very place he impetuously wanted to call down fire on those who refused to hear the gospel. Apparently, something happened. As John spent more time with Jesus, his viewpoint changed. Being exposed to Jesus' extravagant love changed John.

One day Jesus told His disciples the secret of His love for them: "As the Father has loved Me, I also have loved you..." (John 15:9). What an amazing promise! John received a revelation from Jesus that the Lord loved him just as much as the Father loved Jesus. In addition, the same promise applies to you and me. Imagine that! We are totally loved by God!

Secure to serve

John also learned how to humbly serve. Jesus asked him to prepare the Passover supper,[10] and he did it willingly. From this, we can see the complete transformation of grace on his life. He was no longer asking for special favors, but instead was willing to serve. Like John, we need to be willing to serve the Lord in any capacity in which He asks us. When we know God loves us unconditionally, we will be willing to do whatever He says and serve wherever He wants.

The Lord taught John that love knew no bounds and should be extended even to those initially antagonistic to the gospel—like the Samaritans. Getting to know Jesus intimately caused John to love as Jesus loved—unconditionally and fully. John wrote the first, second and third epistles of John, and they are sometimes called the "books of love" because they are written from the heart of a father. By this time in his life, John was thoroughly secure in his Father's love. Even when John was exiled to the Isle of Patmos later in his life, where he wrote the book of Revelation, he did not complain because he knew God loved him! Jesus molded John into a revered and loved disciple.

Secure when facing discouragement

During the early 1990's, I went through a season when I felt like a failure in ministry and leadership. Although I had served as the pastor of a rapidly growing church, I wanted to quit. With all of the outward success, I was tired, felt unappreciated and misunderstood. I felt it would be much easier to leave church leadership behind and go back into the business world.

In the midst of my struggle, I stopped in to see Steve Prokopchak, our staff counselor. I asked him for his evaluation as to why I was not able to lead in a way that some on our team felt was appropriate. Steve gently offered me some kind advice, and then encouraged me to listen to a cassette tape that he felt would be helpful.

A few days later, as I was driving down the road, I popped the cassette into my tape player to see what the speaker had to say. The speaker immediately caught my attention. He started speaking about leaders who have a "messiah complex," feeling they need to have all the answers and be everyone's savior. I was glued to the speaker's words.

Then it dawned on me, I was the speaker on the tape! I rarely listened to myself on tape and had not immediately recognized my own voice. It all came back to me—I had taught a pastors' training course at our church a year before, and on this cassette tape I was encouraging these future pastors to recognize the Lord as the only One who can ultimately meet their needs. I had not taken my own medicine, and I was paying for it!

At Steve's advice and the affirmation of the leadership team of our church, I took a three-month's sabbatical. It took me about five weeks to just feel like a real person again. But during these three months off, I received the revelation from the Lord that my entire significance and security did not come from what I did or from what people thought of me, but instead it came from the fact that Jesus loved me, period! God loved me just because He loved me, not because of what I did!

Secure whether or not other people affirm us

Although I had known this to be theologically correct for years, it had never really sunk into my spirit. The song I had learned as a child: "Jesus loves me this I know, for the Bible tells me so" took on new meaning to me. I was changed! Whether or not people liked me or affirmed me was no longer an issue (of course it is still nice when they do), because I knew God loved me!

I keenly remember pacing back and forth in a cabin in the mountains during this time of my sabbatical, reading aloud from the scriptures over and over again: "I have chosen you and have not cast you away: Fear not, for I am with you; be not be dismayed, for I am your God. I will strengthen you, yes, I will help you, I will uphold you with My righteous right hand...For I, the Lord your God, will hold your right hand, saying to you, 'Fear not, I will help you'" (Isaiah 41:9b,10,13).

During this time of near burnout and disillusionment, the greatest revelation I received from the Lord was that He loved me. Period. He had not rejected me. Regardless of what others may have felt about me (real or imagined), He still loved me! I learned that my significance comes from His love for me, and from His love for me alone. I was now whole because I had personally experienced the Father's love in a new way, so that I could become a spiritually and emotionally healthy spiritual father to others. I did not need the affirmation of others; I had already received the affirmation of my Father in heaven.

Jesus' love relationship with His disciple John displays the unequivocal importance of developing a close friendship with God. And it all starts with us knowing that "Jesus loves me, this I know, for the Bible tells me so." It is so simple, yet so powerful!

Secure and forgiven

Mark must have known that Jesus loved him, but like us, it appears as if he did not always understand the perfect love of Jesus. In the Garden of Gethsemane when things got rough, fear caused him to desert Jesus, along with the other disciples when the mob came to take Jesus away.[11] Another time, Mark deserted Paul, the apostle, on his first missionary trip.[12] Therefore, at the start of another missionary journey, Paul refused to allow Mark to accompany him. This caused a rift between Barnabas and Paul,[13] with Paul rejecting Mark and Barnabas choosing to take Mark with him.

Imagine being the person responsible for splitting up the greatest missionary church planting team in the New Testament! Nevertheless, somewhere along the way, Mark experienced his heavenly Father's love as well as the love of his spiritual fathers—Barnabas and Peter. Apparently, Mark later changed his conduct and Paul forgave his wavering ways, telling the Colossian church to welcome Mark.[14] Later Paul asks for Mark to come to help him,[15] showing that he was reconciled to him.

Secure and useful in God's service

I believe Mark changed from a deserter to a faithful and useful servant of Christ because he received a revelation that Jesus loved him unconditionally. It helped that he also had a praying mother; her house was home for many praying people,[16] including Peter, another of Mark's spiritual fathers (Peter calls him a "son"[17]). It appears as if Mark lived in a single parent home, because his natural father is never mentioned and the scriptures only speak of his mother's home.

The combination of a growing intimacy with the Father and the nurturing aspect of spiritual fathers in Mark's life caused him to grow up spiritually. When we become intimate with our heavenly Father and are willing to be encouraged by faithful mentors, we too will be molded into the kind of people useful for service in God's kingdom. Knowing the Father changes us and matures us into spiritual adulthood. Experiencing His love causes us to grow from spiritual babies, to spiritual young men and women, and encourages us to take the next step to becoming spiritual parents. We can be eternally grateful that Mark did not quit. Because he experienced the Father's unconditional love, he gave us the book of Mark! This is the only book of the four gospels that records Jesus powerful words, "...these signs will follow those who believe..." (Mark 16:17).

Secure to give love away

It is not enough to know that the key to being a spiritual father is to experience His perfect love. We must also be willing to give that love away just as God did: "God so loved the world that He gave..." Giving love away helps us to live up to our full potential in God. It releases the joy of the Lord in our lives! How do we give love away? We give love away by modeling God's love as we point our spiritual children to Jesus. In this way, love can be multiplied through them.

When our spiritual children see that we know the Father, they will want that same loving relationship for themselves. In this role, spiritual fathers and mothers *show* their sons and daughters the Father in heaven. They see, by our prayer life and intimacy with the Lord, that we are in love with Jesus. They will want to experience firsthand the blessed reality of knowing their heavenly Father loves them.

It is a divine privilege to model the love of Jesus. But we must be careful our spiritual children do not rely on us more than they rely on Jesus. Years ago, before I ever heard of the term "spiritual fathering," I mentored some young men who wanted to grow in their new Christian lives. However, out of my zealousness, I provided too much security for them, rather than allowing them to discover how to place their total trust in Jesus. They started looking to me for that which only our Father in heaven could give them. Our mentoring relationship became an unhealthy bondage.

Looking to any leader for all the answers and putting him up on a spiritual pedestal is dangerous, because he is likely to fall off at one point or another! No wonder those I mentored become disillusioned and wounded; I did not have all the answers and I made mistakes.

I learned a valuable lesson about the delicate balance of pointing people to the Father while mentoring them to grow spiritually. We can mentor effectively only if we rely totally on God's grace and constantly direct our spiritual children to Jesus. In this way, they become entirely dependent on Him, not us.

We can never get our emotional and spiritual needs met by the love of a spiritual father. We must know our heavenly Father and experience His love and unconditional acceptance. Similarly, we can never get our needs met by the affirmation of our spiritual sons and daughters. These wrong expectations cause dysfunctional spiritual parenting. We must trust the Father in heaven for His affirmation.

My wife can never completely meet my needs: only Jesus can. However, as I am fulfilled in Him, our relationship takes on a new level of mutual blessing and love.

In the same way, we must have a vital relationship with our heavenly Father to be effective as spiritual parents, or we will minister out of a wrong spirit. The most important role of a spiritual father or mother is to direct others to Jesus!

A close personal relationship with Jesus will keep our spiritual children safe from harm, because their foundation will be strong. Charles Spurgeon once said, "The sheep are never so safe from the wolf as when they are near the shepherd."

Strive for a healed relationship with your natural father

Recently, while visiting in the home of a well-known Christian leader now in his seventies, I asked him, "You have been a spiritual father for years. I am 25 years younger than you. What is one thing that you could tell me now that could be significant as I reach out to help others?"

He did not even hesitate. "I would not place anyone in leadership unless I knew they had a healed relationship with their earthly father. There is a direct relationship between our relationship with our earthly father, and our ability to be a spiritual father." Our relationship with our parents greatly affects our present and future relationships.

Family counselors' offices are filled with people struggling with what happened in their relationships with their parents. Some of us have grown up in dysfunctional homes and have been hurt or abused by earthly parents. Nevertheless, when we come to Christ, we begin a new relationship with a new father—our heavenly Father. Our heavenly Father is not dysfunctional! He will never take advantage of us. He always loves us and believes in us unconditionally!

In the next two chapters, we will look at dysfunctions that hinder us from healthy spiritual fathering and discover how to receive healing to restore us back to the Father and into healthy father-son and mother-daughter relationships.

Notes

1. John 13:23
2. John 19:26
3. John 20:2
4. John 21:7
5. John 21:20-23
6. Mark 3:17
7. Luke 9:54
8. Mark 10:35-45
9. Luke 9:49-50
10. Luke 22:8
11. Mark 14:50
12. Acts 13:13
13. Acts 15:38-40
14. Colossians 4:10
15. II Timothy 4:11
16. Acts 12:12
17. I Peter 5:13

CHAPTER 7

Hindrances To
Spiritual Fathering

What keeps us from experiencing
authentic relationships?

One Saturday morning my six-year-old daughter Leticia begged me to make her pancakes for breakfast. Her mother and sisters were gone for the morning, and she was stuck with me as the potential cook for the family. With my cooking skills being what they are, I pleaded with her, "Please, Leticia, couldn't you just eat cereal today?" She persisted, so I obliged. Half asleep, I read the instructions incorrectly, and the end product looked unfit for human consumption! I asked her again to please eat cereal. She again staunchly persisted. This time the oil in the pan caught on fire! We had to later repaint the blackened spot the fire left on the ceiling. It was not the start to a good day.

"Please try again, Daddy," Leticia implored me with her big blue eyes. How could I resist? I decided just to ignore the instructions. This time, without following the recipe on the side of the box, I got milk and eggs out of the refrigerator and began to mix any ingredients I could find that I thought would work. Amazingly enough, the concoction looked edible. Thankfully, I slid the golden pancakes, with lots of syrup, onto a plate and placed them in front of Leticia. I will never forget her response. She took one bite of my freshly made pancakes, looked up at me with a mixture of despair and disappointment in her eyes and said, "Daddy, may I have cereal, please?"

Leticia grew tired of watching her daddy try to make pancakes over and over again and, because of misreading the directions, not producing edible results. She eventually gave up and decided to go back to something "safe" and easy—cereal! Today, I meet people throughout the body of Christ who have given up because of complicated and unpredictable situations that have come up in spiritual parenting relationships. Any person who is a natural parent knows that raising healthy children has its difficulties. Parents do not bring their children to a place of maturity without some failures along the way.

Sometimes spiritual fathers and mothers, and sons and daughters, too, find themselves in discordant relationships and quit. It is not that the spiritual parents did not try. Perhaps they read the scriptural directions wrongly, and the relationship with their son or daughter flopped. Or maybe a spiritual son or daughter was mentored by a spiritual parent who sought to control rather than encourage. These relationships will finally blow up because they are unhealthy. Yet, by giving up entirely on all spiritual parenting relationships because some do not work out is like throwing the baby out with the bath water!

Not living according to the manufacturer's instructions

I believe the church today is filled with people who want to be spiritual parents. They have the desire to influence the future by passing on a godly legacy but they find themselves unable to do so. You could say these people are not living according to the manufacturer's instructions. Hurts from the past, sin, insecurities or dysfunctional role models stunt them spiritually, preventing them from reaching out to others.

It is a fact that people have a tendency to get off track spiritually. I remember playing with a model electric train as a kid, and time and time again the train would round a corner and fly off the track, lying helpless on its side, spinning its wheels. It could not possibly get back on the tracks without outside help. It was only when I picked up the train and gently set it on the tracks that it could run again. When we allow Him, our Father God will pick us up when we get derailed spiritually and place us back on track. Only then can we arrive at the destination that God intended for us. The Lord is a great Redeemer! He wants to heal the hurts and help believers recover what Satan has tried to steal from them.

Not believing the past can be redeemed and restored

In the first chapter of Matthew, we read the genealogy of Jesus. Why was this very long list of "begats" included in God's Word? This was included for a number of reasons, including that it demonstrates that people, specifically families, are important to God. It also shows that a family can learn from both the successes and failures of its members.

Jesus' genealogy includes Rahab, a former prostitute who delivered the wicked city of Jericho to the Israelites. Her salvation is evidence that God redeems and restores future generations when even one individual turns to God in faith. Even an ungodly family member can be redeemed and the entire next generation can be turned to the Lord.

We must build on the shoulders of those who have gone before us, regardless of the mistakes they may have made. We need to live in a posture of praise to the Lord for those who birthed us and nourished us both naturally and spiritually. We have to purpose in our hearts that, by the grace of God, we will be a positive influence to the next generation.

God wants families to pass on a blessing to the next generation. The Bible is a book recorded for the generations. It is a record of the rich inheritance of relationships down through the generations. God honors and places importance on a family's lineage because each family has a unique story to tell. The people included in Jesus' genealogy had a part in seeing Jesus trained and fathered for thirty years on earth. God the Father put Jesus on loan to Joseph and Mary so they could train him. Jesus' "foster" father, Joseph, trained him in a carpenter's shop. In order for Joseph to be obedient to train Jesus, there had to be faithful individuals in his lineage who passed on a legacy of training. The life of Jesus was based on previous generations and had a direct bearing on His ministry.

In the same way, if we are to pass on an "inheritance" to others, we must receive a spiritual blessing from generations past. We need healthy spiritual fathers and mothers to deposit a rich inheritance into spiritual sons and daughters.

Spiritual parents should expect their spiritual children to grow far beyond them spiritually, just as Jesus expected His followers to go further than He went: "Most assuredly, I say to you, he who believes in Me, the works that I do he will do also; and greater works than these he will do..." (John 14:12). Jesus knew His followers would have an even greater scope of ministry than He had. Thousands of converts would be produced in the first century of the church making a deep impression on mankind. God is a Father who expects His children of each generation to pass on a spiritual inheritance that has an increasingly far-reaching effect and scope.

Not passing on what God has given us

If spiritual blessings are not passed on to our spiritual children, the next generation is in danger of losing everything. When God's people took possession of the Promised Land, they served the Lord as long as the leaders set good examples for them and gave them godly instructions. But when Joshua and the elders of that generation died, the children of Israel forgot the mercies of God to Israel: "When all that generation had been gathered to their fathers, another generation arose after them who did not know the Lord nor the work which He had done for Israel" (Judges 2:10).

Apparently, Joshua and the elders had not trained others to pass on a continuing spiritual legacy. Without spiritual fathers to remind them of what the Lord had done for them when He brought them out of Canaan, the people turned away from God. They no longer remembered or cared about the nation's covenant to obey the Law of the Lord. A spiritual legacy was lost to the next generation because no one had "trained them, to train others..." which is the essence of spiritual parenting.

In his book, *Disciple*, Juan Carlos Ortiz says leaders must know how to release their people so they can grow spiritually:

> But you know what happens in the modern church? We pastors stop somewhere along the way; we know how to administrate, to help, to have some healings, or even teach—but then we stop moving. We become corks. The sheep grow and grow and start jamming up behind us, unable to grow further until we grow some more ourselves. They keep listening to our sermons, and soon they know everything we know, and then we have nothing but a pressure chamber.
>
> The pastor is not a cork intentionally; he is a victim of the

structure like everyone else. It's always been done that way. If the pressure becomes great enough, the pastor gets uncomfortable enough to ask the bishop for a transfer. So the bishop takes out one cork and replaces him with another!

If it is a congregational denomination that doesn't have bishops, the problem is even worse. The pressure keeps building until the channel finally explodes and the cork flies out! He gets really banged up in the explosion, of course, sometimes so badly that he can no longer continue in the ministry.

All this is avoided, of course, if the pastor keeps on growing to apostleship and the sheep keep growing right behind him.

If a pastor is truly a father to his congregation, he cannot be changed (or exploded) every two or three years. What family changes fathers every two years? Maybe our churches are more like clubs that elect presidents for a certain term and then elect someone else. But if we are family, we are a family, we stay together. The father keeps turning over responsibility to his sons [and daughters] as they grow.[1]

Only a dysfunctional parent would keep his grown children at home in order to pay the bills when they are ready to marry and build a home of their own. A normal parent encourages his or her children to go and establish their own homes! In the same way, any spiritual leader who uses the people he should be serving to fulfill his own personal vision is dysfunctional. That means he is not functioning as a proper leader. Sadly, there are many in the church that find themselves confused because they have been hurt in the past by this kind of leadership.

My fifteen-year-old son Josh is responsible to mow the lawn each week, but this is not why the Lord gave him to me! He is being consistently trained now so that he will be motivated to mow his own lawn in the future. We must pass on a healthy legacy to our spiritual children so they will be motivated to do the same.

Waiting until our needs are met

Don't wait until you find a spiritual father or mother—become one yourself! Waiting to get that wonderful spiritual father or mother who will nurture and love you perfectly before you reach out and parent others is like saying (of your natural childhood), "My childhood was terrible. I grew up in a mixed up family, so I can never have kids because I would be a terrible father." This is simply not true! Each parent can begin with a clean slate. Parents must decide to learn from the past and make good choices along the way. If we wait until we receive all the spiritual nurturing we feel we need before we reach out to others, we will never become spiritual parents ourselves.

The scriptures tell us to: "Cast your bread upon the waters, for you will find it after many days" (Ecclesiastes 11:1). Reaching out to parent another may look like you are throwing away your chance for having your own needs met, but by sowing into others' lives, we are promised to reap a return. After having experienced the lack of a spiritual father in my life for about ten years, I made the decision to be a spiritual father to others. And amazingly enough, as I reached out to others and became a spiritual father to them, the Lord brought spiritual fathers into my own life.

The Lord is a great Redeemer. He is waiting for us to stand up and be used even if we have a lot more to learn. God will take us right where we are at and then use us. We cannot afford to stunt our spiritual growth and languish on the sidelines. We may as well give ourselves room to make some mistakes, because we probably will!

Do you know any natural parents who have not made any mistakes? Of course not! Yet, God gives grace to parents who place their faith and confidence in Him. The Lord will be there to cover the blunders you may make as a spiritual parent.

We can make a difference for generations to come if we break the curse of the past and move on to model Jesus' example of spiritual parenting. I meet many Christians today who lacked a decent role model for fathering. Although they witnessed dysfunctional, faulty father images while growing up, they allowed the Lord to mold them into godly role models for their own children. They broke from their past!

A negative parenting role model is no excuse for us to continue to pass on bad parenting. God is a Father to the fatherless (Psalm 68:5). He loves us and will teach us to be healthy parents. As we pour our lives into people, and love them with the love of Jesus, we will begin to model positive family patterns.

What hinders you?

In the following paragraphs, let's look at areas that keep people from developing into spiritual fathers and mothers. Think about your own life. What are some of the things that hinder you from becoming a spiritual father or mother? If you find yourself in one of these categories, don't sit passively by. Endeavor to do what it takes to become a spiritual father or mother. You can help fill the desperate need. You can pass on to your natural and spiritual children a spiritual legacy and have a continuing impact on future generations.

Ignorance keeps many from becoming spiritual fathers or mothers today. Many dedicated Christian believers either never heard of spiritual parenting or they do not understand its concept. Paul told the church at Athens that God overlooks ignorance, but when the truth is made known, people need to repent and change their ways: "Truly, these times of ignorance God overlooked, but now commands all men everywhere to repent" (Acts 17:30). Today's church needs to wake up to the need for spiritual parenting. When we finally understand that God is a God of families and wants each person simply to be a spiritual dad or mom to another person(s), we understand spiritual fathering. No longer ignorant, we are now responsible!

I was ministering at a church, teaching on the truths of spiritual parenting and cell group ministry, when a young lawyer came to me after the meeting. He said enthusiastically, "I want to be a spiritual parent. It all makes sense. I can do that! I can be a spiritual father to a small group of people who want to grow in God." I encouraged him to speak to his pastor about his desire to serve in this way. I later spoke to the lawyer's pastor, and told him of the young man's enthusiasm.

The pastor said with a big smile, "I've been trying to get him to take leadership of a small group of believers for a long time!" At last, the young man had his spiritual eyes opened to spiritual parenting. He had received a revelation of spiritual parenting from the Lord!

Jesus asked His disciples: "Who do men say that I, the Son of Man, am?"

Peter replied, "You are the Christ, the Son of the living God."

Jesus then told Peter clearly: "...flesh and blood has not revealed this to you, but My Father who is in heaven" (Matthew 16:13,16,17).

In the same way that Peter received a revelation from his Father in heaven, we each need a revelation from the Lord regarding spiritual parenting, or we just set up a new "spiritual parenting program." Becoming a spiritual father and mother is a life message, not a new church program.

This young lawyer now saw clearly that he did not have to start a program, but he could simply become a "dad." He had faith in his heart that could accomplish it, being aware that dads learn by trial and error as they have kids of their own. He did not have to be perfect, but he would learn along the way. The young lawyer's pastor became a mentor to him—a spiritual father and friend. He went on to learn how to be a spiritual dad as he loved his spiritual children and desired the best for them.

Apathy is another reason for a lack of spiritual fathering today. Many Christians get so caught up in the things of the world: making a living, taking their kids to soccer games, golfing, and participating in civic activities, feeling they have no time to be a spiritual father or mother. As good as these things may be, they do not take the place of the faith-building, deeply satisfying adventure of helping other believers grow in Christ.

When people become wrapped up in their own lives and selfish desires, they become apathetic to the things of God. Revelation 3:19, in the Living Bible, tells us clearly to "turn [repent] from your indifference and become enthusiastic about the things of God."

As we repent of apathy in Jesus' name, the Lord will give us grace and wisdom to take others with us as we go about our daily lives. Jesus called His disciples first and foremost "to be with Him." Our spiritual sons and daughters learn much more by watching us live our lives in Christ before them than by listening to our "sermons." It is easier than you think to accommodate others into your daily activities. How about if you are going to play golf? Take your spiritual son along! If you are going to go shopping, take one of your spiritual daughters with you. I seldom travel alone. I value the time I have with various spiritual sons whom I invite to join me on trips throughout the world.

Insecurity tempts a person to think, "How could God ever use me? I do not know how to be a spiritual parent. I'm afraid. I don't know the Bible well enough. I need to get my life more together." If you feel this way, you have a lot of company.

Moses told the Lord he could not speak properly. Jeremiah told the Lord he was too young. Joshua was scared, and the Lord kept reassuring him to be of good courage and that he would be with him just as he was with his "father" Moses. Gideon thought he was brought up in the wrong family for the Lord to use him. The list goes on and on.

Maybe you did not go to seminary or Bible school, but the little you know is certainly more than the spiritual baby in Christ you are reaching out to. Even Paul, the apostle, admitted to the Corinthian church that he had a deep sense of his own weaknesses that caused him to feel fearful and inadequate: "And I, brethren, when I came to you, did not come with excellence of speech or of wisdom declaring to you the testimony of God...I was with you in weakness, in fear, and in much trembling." (I Corinthians 2:1,3). Nevertheless, Paul goes on to declare that although his speech was not persuasive, the Holy Spirit's power was in his words.

II Timothy 1:7 says it another way, "For God has not given us a spirit of fear, but of power and of love and of a sound mind." Insecurities will keep us paralyzed, and we will never move beyond our comfort zone. However, if we trust God, He will allow us to use our gifts and even increase them to help others. He will give us courage and resolution. God's love will always win over the fear of man.

A lack of modeling may cause us to wait on the sidelines because we have no idea how to parent. Perhaps we never had a parent to guide us—natural or spiritual.

I recently read a book for dads about training their sons to grow up to be men of God. The man who wrote this book tells how he grew up with a dad who was drunk most of the time. He had a father positionally, but emotionally his father was not involved in his life. The author refused to allow his painful childhood to be an excuse not to be a good father to his own children. When he came to Christ and later had children of his own, he made a commitment to train a whole new generation of fathers to train their sons for God. Today, as a writer and pastor, he uses his platform to explain how the curse of a dysfunctional family can be broken when a person comes to Christ and walks in freedom. We cannot allow our perceptions to be distorted by poorly modeled examples. By faith, we must press on and overcome so we can demonstrate to our children a better way.

Remember, God is a perfect Father! He is the model of a father who loves us perfectly and believes the best about us. No matter what we have done, we are accepted and loved by our heavenly Father.

Impatience will cause us to quit when we don't see quick results. Believing we will have instant success is contrary to the scriptural principle of sowing and reaping. It is often hard work for spiritual fathers or mothers to nurture and train spiritual babies before they can grow up to care for themselves and eventually become spiritual parents.

There are three stages to the fulfillment of any vision, including the vision to become an effective spiritual parent: (1) the honeymoon stage, (2) the trial (test) stage where you feel like quitting, and (3) the fruitfulness stage.

The Bible is filled with examples of those who started with an exciting vision, refused to quit during the trial stage, and then experienced great fruitfulness. The story of Joseph is one of the best. After having a dream that his brothers would bow down to him, he encountered trial after trial. Joseph was sold as a slave by his brothers, lied about by his employer's wife, imprisoned while innocent, forgotten in prison, and yet he became second in command of all of Egypt overnight! He entered the stage of great fruitfulness as he refused to give up during the hard season of his life.

God used this stage of trial in Joseph's life to make him into the man of character He had called him to be. He could then be a blessing to his brothers who had treated him so wrongly just a few years before. Joseph passed the test! Many quit during the test period and never experience the stage of fruitfulness the Lord has planned for them.

The Lord is much more concerned about what He is doing in you than about you reaching your final goal in your spiritual parenting relationship. He wants you to depend on Him and on His power in the here and now. Oswald Chambers once said, "If I can stay calm, faithful, and unconfused while in the middle of the turmoil of life, the goal of the purpose of God is being accomplished in me. God is not working toward a particular finish—His purpose is the process itself."[2] The

Lord is calling us to complete dependency on Him as we persevere in our parenting relationships.

Fear of our mistakes can hinder us. Bob Mumford once said, "I do not trust anyone unless he walks with a limp." I often feel the same way about those whom I meet. Jacob, after wrestling with the Lord and demanding His blessing, was touched in his thigh and received the Lord's blessing. But from that day on, he walked with a limp. When God lovingly deals with us in the difficult times, we walk with a spiritual limp the rest of our lives. This is the stuff true spiritual fathers are made of.

When I was young, I thought I had all of the answers. Now, as I turn 50 this year, I realize how much I do not know. I am totally convinced that if God does not show up, it is all over for me! But it is such a good place to be!

Peter, Jesus' disciple who became an apostle of the New Testament church, after denying Jesus, and experiencing His complete acceptance and forgiveness, lost his abrasiveness and became a true father in the faith. He now "walked with a limp."

Many times, we make our share of mistakes while parenting. But we cannot become weary. We may be doing all the right things, but problems still arise. We may be tempted to go back to something easier than dealing with the shortcomings of humanity. Spiritual fathering and mothering is not easy. However, it is rewarding. Even Jesus dealt with problems while fathering the twelve. They all left Him in the Garden of Gethsemane. He felt alone and forsaken. But He knew the last chapter was not yet written! Fifty days later, Peter stood with the eleven and preached at Pentecost, and three thousand people came to faith in Christ. The New Testament church began to grow exponentially.

Hurts from the past hinder some from developing into a spiritual father or mother: "I've tried to be a spiritual dad to someone, and I was hurt. I don't want to be hurt again." Well, I have news for you—you probably will get hurt again! If you are a natural parent, you will know that you sometimes experience pain and disappointment as you raise your kids. With spiritual kids, taking initiative requires taking risks. They will not always like what you have to say. They can be tiresome or forget appointments. They may sometimes act like they don't care.

Paul, the apostle, a spiritual father to many, tells us in II Timothy 4:16, that his children abandoned him when he was in a real pinch. He had to appear before the emperor, and the Christians at Rome were afraid, so they deserted him: "At my first defense no one stood with me, but all forsook me. May it not be charged against them."

Paul could have been deeply hurt from the abandonment of his followers, but he chose to not count it against them. Jesus' followers abandoned Him too. They ran in terror into the night when the mob came with their torches and weapons to take Jesus in the Garden of Gethsemane. But Christ forgave them. Even God, Himself, was abandoned by one third of his staff when Lucifer rebelled and was thrown out of heaven.

The inconsistent or irritating behavior in our spiritual children may come from a deep struggle in their lives to overcome a stubborn sin. Don't throw in the towel just yet. Look beyond the superficial symptoms and be willing to take the risk to challenge your spiritual son or daughter to face his or her problem and then lay it at the foot of the cross. After all, it is God's problem. Trust Him to raise His child His way. You are only responsible to be a consistent and gentle coach.

You may have some discouraging and frustrating times as a spiritual parent, but you will learn to lean wholly on the Lord. The last chapter in your son or daughter's life has not yet been written. Spiritual fathering and mothering is an ongoing legacy that bears fruit through consistent, loving cultivation.

Abuse of authority can warp the entire concept of spiritual fathering and mothering. Spiritual fathers and mothers are not dominating authority figures that coerce their children into submission. They must tread lightly as they point their spiritual children to Jesus. I like how Floyd McClung describes the much needed balance we need to exercise in the area of spiritual fathering and mothering in his book, *The Father Heart of God*:

> Godly fathers want to serve others, and treat all men and women as their equals. Their actions proceed from an attitude of equality, not authority, because they are more concerned with serving than ruling. The following chart helps point out the differences between the two approaches:

Dominating Fathers	**Fathers in the Lord**
1. Function as if they are the source of guidance for people's lives.	1. Believe that God is the source of guidance and desire to help other Christians learn to hear His voice.
2. Emphasize the rights of leaders.	2. Emphasize the responsibilities of leaders.
3. Set leaders apart and give them special privileges.	3. Emphasize the body of Christ serving one another.
4. Seek to control people's actions.	4. Encourage people to be dependent on God.
5. Emphasize the importance of the leaders ministering to others.	5. Emphasize the importance of equipping the saints for the work of the ministry.
6. Use rules and laws to control people and force them to conform to a mold.	6. Provide an atmosphere of trust and grace to encourage growth.

Biblical authority is never taken; it is offered...It comes from the anointing of God's Spirit and is the sum total of one's character, wisdom, spiritual gift, and servant attitude. Fathers in the Lord understand these principles about authority. They know the character of the Father, so they are relaxed in their ministry to other people...they have learned to take action as God directs, and not just because they are "the leader."[3]

Healthy spiritual fathers earn the right to speak into their sons' lives because they do so with the heart of a servant, affirming and encouraging them in their walk with Christ. A level of trust is built over time in a balanced relationship that encourages sons and daughters to be dependent on God.

Perhaps you feel hindered by some of the experiences you had as you grew up spiritually. Maybe you were abused, hurt, disappointed, held back, or lacked a healthy role model to follow. The Lord has a great plan for you! You can be restored!

In the next chapter we will look at how our Lord is restoring His people. He is placing the "burned stones" back on His wall of service as healed, completely functional and restored spiritual parents.

Notes

[1] Juan Carlos Ortiz, *Disciple,* (Florida: Creation House, 1975), p. 97.

[2] Oswald Chambers, *My Utmost For His Highest,* (Grand Rapids, Michigan: Discovery House, 1992), July 28.

[3] Floyd McClung, *The Father Heart of God*, (Eugene, Oregon: Harvest House Publishers, 1985), pp. 129-131.

CHAPTER 8

Can These Burned
Stones Live?

God places discouraged fathers and
mothers back on His wall of service

The enemies of God's people ridiculed Nehemiah and his workers
as they started to rebuild the wall around Jerusalem. The wall had
been broken down for ages and the stones were charred and useless. How did these people think they could do anything with the mess?
"Can these burned stones live?" they mocked (Nehemiah 4:2). They
did not want to see Jerusalem become secure and safe again, because
they wanted to continue to run roughshod over its boundaries.

The devil is throwing similar accusations at God's people today:
"How does that Christian think he can function with all the baggage he
carries around from that broken relationship he had with his father?"
or "You've made too many mistakes, how do you expect to help someone else?"

Perhaps we sincerely tried reaching out to another and the relationship deteriorated so we feel like a failure. Maybe a person helping
us (a spiritual father we looked up to) used control and legalism to get
his point across. Devastated and hurt, we tell ourselves we will never
place ourselves in a position to be hurt again. The devil wants to rob us
of hope so he can keep us defeated and discouraged.

Believe God, not the lies of the enemy

We cannot believe the lies of the enemy and expect to live victoriously. If we justify our current negative situation by blaming it on past bad experiences, we will wallow in bitterness and unforgiveness. As spiritual parents, if we feel unable to fulfill the Lord's call on our lives because we have believed the lies of the enemy, we will be spiritually paralyzed. We must believe that, although our own resources are few, we can carry out God's work because we are going to trust in the overruling providence of God. The burned stones were charred and looked useless, but God's people chose not to look at the dismal circumstances. Because they refused to listen to their enemies' discouraging words, they succeeded in rebuilding the wall.

Mephibosheth was a young man who lived the first part of his life believing a lie. He hid out in the town of Lo Debar, believing his life was in great danger. Since his grandfather, Saul, was no longer the king of Israel, he was told it was only a matter of time until David, the new king, found him. He had been told the stories about the new king and how that, for generations, whenever a new king came into power, all family members of the former king were decapitated.

Mephibosheth lived, not only in emotional pain, but physical pain as well. While still a small child, he was crippled when a servant girl dropped him as they were fleeing from the new king advancing toward the palace. He was emotionally and physically scarred, and like the stones of the fallen wall around Jerusalem, he appeared "burned"—unable to fulfill his destiny.

One dreaded day, the new king's servants arrived in Lo Debar to find the grandson of King Saul. When they brought him to the palace, Mephibosheth fell on his face in terror and prostrated himself before the king. Mephibosheth couldn't believe his ears when he heard the king say, "...Do not fear, for I will surely show you kindness for Jonathan your father's sake, and will restore to you all the land of Saul your grandfather; and you shall eat bread at my table continually" (II Samuel 9:7).

Unknown to Mephibosheth, David had made a covenant with Mephibosheth's father Jonathan years before. They had pledged to take care of each other's families if anything ever happened to them. When Jonathan was killed in battle with his father Saul, David remembered his covenant with his best friend Jonathan. He was committed to keeping his promise!

For years, Mephibosheth had believed a lie. He was convinced that David would kill him, but all the while David was pursuing him and had his best interests at heart. Mephibosheth was esteemed by David and given the honor of sitting at the king's table. Every need Mephibosheth had was completely met.

What if you were "burned or dropped"?

Like Mephibosheth, did you ever feel someone "dropped" you, crippling you for life? I meet so many people with a clear call of God on their lives, who feel they have been burned emotionally or dropped by someone they trusted. Some were burned by a relationship deteriorating after spending a lot of time developing it. In other cases, they were disillusioned when a natural father or a spiritual father disappointed them, so they gave up. They often live in deep disappointment and fear that the Lord will never be able to use them again.

Not too many years ago, Cedric, now leading a thriving church in East Africa, felt burned. He worked side by side with a missionary and planted nearly 400 churches in his native country, looking to this man as a spiritual father. The relationship began to unravel when Cedric started to notice that money was the bottom line for the missionary. The missionary cared little about the souls brought to the Lord through church planting; he was motivated by financial gain. Cedric attempted to untangle himself from the missionary's web of deception and greed, narrowly escaping harm when the missionary sent thugs to burn Cedric's house down. Shell-shocked and grieved, Cedric moved to a neighboring nation and enrolled in a university. While there, he fellowshipped at a church where people reached out in love to him. As he was restored, he again took a step of faith to take up his mantle as a spiritual father. God began to use him as a leader in small group ministry, and he later returned to his native country to plant a church. He was willing to start over because he refused to be intimidated by Satan's discouraging lies. This burned stone was healed! Today, Cedric is serving as a spiritual father to other pastors in his nation.

Drink the cup

Are you a burned stone? Maybe you think you made a mistake from which you never will recover. Maybe you tried reaching out to someone and they ripped you off. Perhaps, like Cedric, a spiritual parent has hurt you, and you feel misunderstood or wrongly accused.

God's Word cautions us from trying to vindicate ourselves when others accuse us falsely. Instead, we should "drink the cup" and the Lord will vindicate us as illustrated in Numbers 5:11-20. In the Old Testament, a man who suspected his wife of adultery brought her to the priest where she was given dirty water to drink from a cup. If she was guilty, she would get sick and diseased and become a curse among her people, but if she was innocent, the Lord would vindicate her. She would be fruitful and bear children. Either way, she had to drink the cup!

God knows our hearts. He knows the truth. It does not help to try to prove our innocence on our own. He has to do it. Our role needs to be one of forgiveness, otherwise we will harbor resentment.

The Bible says there are two types of ministries before the throne of God—the ministry of intercession and the "ministry" of accusation. Jesus intercedes before the Father for us, but the devil accuses us. If Satan uses someone to lie about us, although it is tempting to lash out and try to vindicate ourselves, we should simply "drink the cup," in a spirit of humility and forgiveness. God is the vindicator.

A former co-laborer in church leadership, who left our church several years ago, recently met with me and one of my colleagues. The Lord had spoken to him and challenged him concerning which of these two ministries he was embracing. To his surprise, he realized he was participating in a "ministry" of accusation against the church. It had crippled him and robbed his joy. The Lord convicted him of his judgmental spirit and he sincerely repented. Today, this precious man of God is one of our personal intercessors. The Lord is so redemptive!

Mercy triumphs over judgment

Spiritual fathers and mothers in the body of Christ must grasp this simple, important truth: We need to forgive others just as we want to be forgiven. We must extend mercy to each other and leave the judgment to God (Luke 6:37). Mercy always triumphs over judgment! (James 2:13). Mercy is giving what is not deserved. It is letting someone off the hook because of love. We must be quick to extend mercy to the struggler.

Satan accuses the one struggling, "Can you, as a burned stone, live?"

Jesus is answering us loudly and clearly. "Yes, I will restore you and place you back on My wall for service in My kingdom."

We cannot look at our natural circumstances and give up. Our God is a God who forgives and restores burned stones. Mercy really illustrates what God is like. Our merciful Lord wants to restore these who have been burned because of sin, bad role models, or by not responding properly to tests the Lord allowed in their lives. He wants us back in fellowship with Him and others.

According to I Peter 2:5, as Christians, we are living stones, being built together into a spiritual house—the body of Christ. And we are built together by the mortar of relationships: "You also, as living stones, are being built up a spiritual house, a holy priesthood, to offer up spiritual sacrifices acceptable to God through Jesus Christ." Every living stone is touching other living stones. We were not created to live the Christian life alone. We are called to be in relationship with one another. When we are burned by others through disappointment, unmet expectations, or spiritual abuse, we can feel like burned stones. Nevertheless, the Lord is redemptive! He takes burned stones, heals them, and places them back on the wall of service for Him.

I know first hand what it feels like. I felt like a burned stone for a period of time I served as a pastor. I nearly quit. I felt misunderstood by those I believed I had given my life for, and I felt unable to do anything about it. Here is how I described what I was going through in my book, *House to House*:

> During the spring of 1992, I was ready to quit. I felt misunderstood, and I was not sure if it was worth all the hassle. I told LaVerne one day, "If I get kicked in the head one more time (figuratively speaking), I don't know if I can get up again."
>
> As the senior leader of our church, I was frustrated, exhausted and overworked. God had given me a vision to be involved in building the underground church, but in the last few years, we had strayed from that original vision. My immaturity as a leader, lack of training and my own inability to communicate clearly the things that God was showing me led to frustration.

In a misguided attempt to please everyone, I was listening to dozens of voices that seemed to be giving conflicting advice and direction. I felt unable to get back on track. I was tired and was encouraged to take a sabbatical.[1]

It was on that sabbatical that the Lord gave me new direction. I am grateful to the Lord that He gave me the grace to continue and to believe again. Today, I am so fulfilled as the Lord has placed me back on His wall of service for Him. Since that time, the Lord placed spiritual fathers in my life to encourage me. Knowing the incredible value of spiritual fathering has changed my life! It is my life's mission to be obedient to Him to serve others and train others to become spiritual parents. I am so blessed the Lord would not allow me to quit. I am having the time of my life. I love my Savior; I love my wife; I love my family; I love the people I work with; I love what I do; it is great to be alive!

Of all of the people that I meet, those who have experienced dysfunctional parenting (both natural and spiritual) seem to be the most fearful of trying to be spiritual parents themselves because they have been burned. But the Lord is touching deeply those who have been burned, healing them completely and then placing them back on the wall of service for Him.

The Father will restore

I love this modern-day story of restoration of a son to his father. It seems that a young man named Sawat disgraced his family and dishonored his father's name, but observe what happened when he refused to listen to the devil's lies anymore:

> Sawat had come to Bangkok to escape the dullness of village life...When he first arrived, he had visited a hotel unlike any he had ever seen. Every room had a window facing into the hallway, and in every room sat a girl...That visit began Sawat's adventure into Bangkok's world of prostitution...Soon he was selling opium to customers and propositioning tourists in the hotels. He even went so low as to actually help buy and sell young girls, some of them only nine and ten years old. It was a nasty business, and he was one of the most important of the young "businessmen."

Then the bottom dropped out of his world: He hit a string of bad luck...and finally ended up living in a shanty by the city trash pile. Sitting in his little shack, he thought about his family, especially his father, a simple Christian man from a small southern village near the Malaysian border. He remembered his dad's parting words: "I am waiting for you." He wondered whether his father would still be waiting for him after all that he had done to dishonor the family name...Word of Sawat's life-style had long ago filtered back to the village.

Finally, he devised a plan. "Dear father," he wrote, "I want to come home, but I don't know if you will receive me after all that I have done. I have sinned greatly, father. Please forgive me. On Saturday night, I will be on the train that goes through our village. If you are still waiting for me, will you tie a piece of cloth on the po tree in front of our house? (Signed) Sawat."

As the train finally neared the village, he churned with anxiety...Sitting opposite him was a kind stranger who noticed how nervous his fellow passenger had become. Finally, Sawat could stand the pressure no longer. He blurted out his story in a torrent of words. As they entered the village, Sawat said, "Oh sir, I cannot bear to look. Can you watch for me? What if my father will not receive me back?"

Sawat buried his face between his knees. "Do you see it, sir? It's the only house with a po tree."

"Young man, your father did not hang just one piece of cloth. Look! He has covered the whole tree with cloth!" Sawat could hardly believe his eyes. The branches were laden with tiny white squares. In the front yard his old father jumped up and down, joyously waving a piece of white cloth, then ran in halting steps beside the train. When it stopped at the little station, he threw his arms around his son, embracing him with tears of joy. "I've been waiting for you!" he exclaimed.

Sawat's story poignantly parallels Jesus' parable of the Prodigal Son, found in Luke 15:11-24. Christ told of another son who threw his life and money away in a whirlwind of wrong choices and fearfully returned home in the hopes that his father would take him back. He too was met with open arms, and was loved and accepted unconditionally.[2]

The Lord awaits those with open arms when they return to Him. He longs to restore us. His forgiveness and acceptance is always extended. We cannot allow Satan to deceive us with his empty promises and fallacious lies.

How to be restored

Do you know that the Bible says Jesus Christ became a curse for us so that we can be set free from the devil's lies over us? "Christ has redeemed us from the curse of the law, having become a curse for us...For this purpose the Son of God was manifested, that He might destroy the works of the devil" (Galatians 3:13; I John 3:8). We can be free from the devil's lies over our lives because we are free from the curse. We do not have to live in bondage.

We live in a fallen world but we were raised with Christ when we were redeemed, or bought back by the blood Jesus shed on the cross two thousand years ago. Jesus came to give us abundant life and set us free (John 8:32). Step by step, we reclaim what Satan has stolen from us—in our homes, in our workplaces, at school—as believers, we have the privilege of pointing the way home to those who are lost. God has a loving plan of redemption for every believer and seeks to accomplish His plan through ordinary people like us.

1. Faith unlocks the door. If we hide behind a locked door, attempting to bulletproof ourselves from hurts, we harden our hearts. God wants to expose and free us. How? It's simple. John 8:32 says that when you believe in Christ, you "shall know the truth, and the truth shall make you free." Jesus Christ, who is Truth, makes men and women free! We become free from being captives to sin—to our false notions, hurts, mistakes and prejudices that entangle and enslave the soul. Now we fall into the arms of Him whose yoke is easy and whose burden is light. We can trust Jesus to restore our lives. As we confess the truth of God's Word, Romans 10:17 says that faith is built. Only then can we begin to experience God's wholeness.

2. Stake your claim. God promised the children of Israel the fertile land of Canaan. It was legally their land because God promised it to them. But they had to receive it by going in, taking it from their enemies, and staking the claim for themselves. The same truth applies to us today. We need to take back the areas of our lives the devil has stolen from us. If the devil has stolen our peace, our joy, our health or our hope; today is our day to claim it back from the enemy! We need to go in and claim back from the devil the specific areas he has stolen from us. When we take Him at His Word, the Lord honors His covenant with us![3]

3. Receive prayer from a trusted friend. For help in your restoration process, you may want to humbly seek the counsel of a godly friend or spiritual parent. He or she can assist you on how to obtain God's forgiveness, receive healing in your emotions, and gain the strength to sin no more.[4]

4. Be patient. The process may not happen overnight. Corrie ten Boom, who experienced life in a Nazi concentration camp, attested to the "ding-dong theory" when it came to finding complete healing. She said that when you ask the Lord to heal and restore you, the devil will try to bring some of the old emotions of hurt and pain back to you again and again. But like the ding-dong of a church bell that rings loud at first and then grows softer and softer until it finally stops ringing, the hurts will grow more faint and distant as you forgive others and claim healing and restoration for your life.

I met a couple in Dallas, Texas, a few years back who desperately wanted to have children. They tried to have a baby for seventeen years and refused to quit believing. The last time I was in Dallas, they were holding their baby boy, after trusting God for seventeen long years. Regardless of your prior experiences, you need to believe again for spiritual children. This means you must allow the Lord to strengthen and season you through the burning process.

5. Keep your branches growing over the wall. God is calling you to be a healthy, functional spiritual parent. Even if you have not had a spiritual parent yourself, the Lord will teach you to be a spiritual parent to the next generation if you keep your eyes on Jesus. Joseph, a man of moral and spiritual strength, was likened to a young fruit tree with its branches going over the well wall (Genesis 49:22). The moisture from the well kept the tree watered and bearing fruit. Your branches will grow abundantly over the wall too if you are constantly watered by the Word of God and the Holy Spirit. You will be sure to bear fruit for Him in the form of many spiritual children when you keep your roots well-watered.

You will be stronger!

Our God is restoring spiritual fathers and mothers to their sons and daughters in these days and gently placing them back on His wall of service. God is calling forth His people in these days who have been burned and broken, and He is healing them and giving them a job to do.

When a metal such as iron is heated in the fire, it is refined and tempered, and it gains great strength. Those who have faced difficulties and allowed God to temper them are refined and ready to be used because they are stronger. For example, couples who are victorious after experiencing marital struggles are just the ones to help other couples who are struggling in their marriage.

You must find your place on the wall. God loves to use burned stones! If you are a burned stone, receive the grace of God today from your heavenly Father to be made whole through His son Jesus Christ. God wants to bless you, make you strong, and give you a great inheritance of spiritual children, as you will learn in the next chapter.

Notes
[1]   Larry Kreider, *House to House* (Ephrata, Pennsylvania: House to House Publications, 1998), p.177.
[2]   The Sawat story is taken from *The Father Heart of God*, Floyd McClung, (Eugene, Oregon: Harvest House Publishers, 1985), pp.111-114.
[3]   Larry Kreider, *Biblical Foundation # 6, Freedom From the Curse*, (Ephrata, Pennsylvania: House to House Publications, 1996), p. 22.
[4]   James 5:16; John 8:11

CHAPTER 9

Collect Your Inheritance!

Leave a legacy of spiritual children

Have you ever heard of the Shakers? They were a religious group that flourished in early 19th century America, building large communities in the eastern United States. Because of their peculiar trembling at their meetings, they were called the Shakers. Today, the Shakers are history. The most visible trace of the group remains in the simple, well-made furniture they manufactured. Why did this once thriving group so rapidly die out? Because of a peculiar theology they practiced: The Shakers believed in, and practiced, celibacy above marriage. They had little opportunity to multiply. Soon, even the religious revivals which had brought many converts to Shakerism lost momentum, and the group declined in the late 1800's.

When a spiritual posterity is stunted like it was for the Shakers, we reproduce no children and our legacy dies. Without raising up spiritual fathers and mothers in our generation, we are in danger of losing the next generation.

My extended family gathers every year for a reunion—aunts, uncles, brothers, sisters, cousins, nephews, and nieces who are all connected to the Kreider family tree. When my grandparents were alive, I noticed how they seemed to look at each other with a twinkle in their eyes at these family gatherings. They knew we were all there because of them, and it gave them deep satisfaction to see their posterity.

The Lord wants to see spiritual families continually reproducing in each generation down through the ages. He has a generational perspective, and we must too. Paul, the apostle, was thinking in terms of four generations when he called Timothy his son and exhorted him to find faithful men to whom he can impart what Paul taught him to the next generation: "And the things you [second generation] have heard from me [first generation] among many witnesses, commit these to faithful men [third generation] who will be able to teach others [fourth generation] also" (II Timothy 2:2).

Paul was thinking about his spiritual posterity and speaking as a spiritual father to his son Timothy who would give him spiritual grandchildren and great grandchildren. The entire Bible was written from a family perspective. It was natural for Paul to think in terms of spiritual posterity because that is how biblical society was set up and the way God intended it to be.

God has called us to birth a spiritual lineage

In Genesis 15:1, when God spoke to Abraham about a promised spiritual seed, He said, "Do not be afraid, Abram. I am your shield, your exceedingly great reward." When God gives us a spiritual revelation to be spiritual parents, we need not be afraid. We may make mistakes or sometimes get hurt by people we are helping, but we have a shield to protect us. God will be our great reward.

Abraham was ninety-nine years old when God gave him the promise that he would be the "father of many nations" (Genesis 17:4). This covenant also promised that his descendants would "multiply as the stars of heaven" (Genesis 26:4).

True, this covenant is speaking about the covenant between God and Abraham and the Jewish people. But Galatians 3:29 says that those who belong to Christ are "Abraham's seed, and heirs according to the promise."

Therefore, as believers, God wants to birth in us "nations," too. These "nations" or groups of people, who come to know God because of our influence, will be our spiritual lineage—they are our posterity in God's kingdom. We have been promised it because we are children of promise. Our God desires to give us a spiritual posterity.

Our inheritance of spiritual children

This promise of spiritual children is for every Christian! God has placed us here on earth because He has called us to become spiritual fathers and mothers in our generation. With this comes the expectation that our spiritual children will have spiritual children and more spiritual children and continue into infinity.

Our inheritance will be all these spiritual children that we can some day present to Jesus Christ. No matter what we do—whether we are a housewife, a student, a worker in a factory, a pastor of a church, or the head a large corporation—we have the divine blessing and responsibility to birth spiritual children, grandchildren and great grandchildren. We are all called to impart to others the rich inheritance that God has promised.

A few years ago, I ministered at a training conference to equip church leaders to become effective spiritual fathers and mothers at a four-year-old church in Lincoln, California, pastored by Daren Laws. I was amazed at what I experienced there. This fledgling church was already 600 people strong and was focusing on training spiritual fathers and mothers to open their homes to minister to young Christians. More than 80% of the people in the church were new believers. Even the mayor and his wife had come to faith in Christ.

When a person came to Christ, he or she was immediately invited to a home church (small group). There the new Christian was connected by relationships into the body of Christ. A spiritual parent nurtured the new believer until he could become a spiritual parent himself, and a new generation of believers was birthed! Daren and his team did not focus on church programs but instead on Jesus and on spiritual parenting.

I like how Abraham responded when the Lord showed him the stars in the heaven and promised him descendants as numerous as the stars: "And he [Abraham] believed in the Lord..." (Genesis 15:6). What did he believe the Lord for? His inheritance! We, too, need to "believe the Lord" for many spiritual children. We can trust God to do it. It may not happen overnight, but it will happen when we trust in God's faithfulness.

One time after ministering at a church in Dallas, Texas, a young man ran up to me holding a Bible, and wanted to tell me his personal testimony: "My folks are not Christians, but recently I opened up this Bible I found laying on the coffee table. After reading in it, I realized I needed Jesus. I gave my life to Christ and then drove around with my Bible in hand looking for a church family. I found a church building near where I lived and walked in.

"The first person to greet me was a young lady, and after telling her my story, she called her father over and said, 'Tell my dad what you told me.'

"The dad listened to my testimony with interest and then examined the Bible I held in my hands. 'Fifteen years ago,' he said, 'I witnessed to a man I served with in the military. He declined to receive the Lord, but agreed to take the Bible you are holding. The man I witnessed to was your father!'"

The young man went on to tell me that he was now preparing to marry the young lady he met at the church building, and they were excited about serving as cell group leaders. Their spiritual lineage would continue. What an awesome story of spiritual posterity in God's kingdom!

We are promised an inheritance of spiritual children. God *wants* to give us an inheritance of spiritual children. And He will do it through the generations. He is a God who has a heart for families and is concerned about the generations to come.

Healthy families will multiply

The Lord wants us to be fruitful and multiply (Genesis 1:28). Our God is a God of multiplication. Multiplication is a fact of nature. As a farm boy, I once counted the kernels on a healthy stalk of corn and found there to be 1200 kernels in the first generation. Do you know that by the next generation there will be one million, four hundred and forty thousand kernels of corn?

In the same way, healthy cells in the body multiply and result in growth of the body. A living cell is in a state of constant activity.

The church in the book of Acts multiplied rapidly because they understood the value of small "cell" groups in homes to aid in nurturing believers through spiritual family relationships. They functioned in close relationship with each other, just as cells in the body function. This healthy activity and interdependence resulted in healthy growth for the early church.

As the Lord restores spiritual family life into His kingdom today, the church in our generation will also multiply rapidly. We must be ready. We must properly train and prepare spiritual parents and sons and daughters so that Christ may be formed in them. Romans 8:19 says, "For the earnest expectation of the creation eagerly waits for the revealing of the sons of God." When Christ is fully formed in His people, creation is even going to sit up and take notice!

Paul was longing to see his spiritual children in Thessalonica and says in I Thessalonians 2:19-20: "For what is our hope, or joy, or crown of rejoicing? Is it not even you in the presence of our Lord Jesus Christ at His coming? For you are our glory and joy." His spiritual children were his glory and joy—his inheritance! Paul rejoiced like a winner receiving a garland of victory (crown) at the games when he thought of his spiritual children and grandchildren that he would present to Christ.

I carry photos of my children and grandson in my wallet. They are my joy and my posterity! When I look at them, I know I had a part in their being on this earth. Our spiritual sons, daughters and grandchildren are our spiritual posterity.

A spiritual legacy

Last year I was in Barbados, training church leaders and believers in many of the churches on the subject of spiritual parenting and cell group ministry. The day I was to leave to come back to the USA, Bill Landis, a missionary living with his family in Barbados who leads *Youth With A Mission's* Caribbean ministry, asked me to his home before going to the airport. Bill and his family, along with a team of leaders, spend their time training and equipping Christians to become spiritual leaders in the Caribbean. On this visit to Barbados, Bill told me some interesting history of this tiny island nation.

He explained that, years ago, many in Barbados came as slaves to the island from West Africa including the nation of The Gambia. Now, after receiving Christ and being trained as missionaries, Barbadians were being sent to their ancestral country of The Gambia to lead Muslim Gambians to Christ. With a common heritage, it was the ideal match. Then he said something that moved me deeply, "Larry, do you realize the people being reached in The Gambia are a part of your spiritual heritage? You were one of my spiritual fathers."

As I sat on the plane returning to the United States, I was dumbfounded at the significance of Bill's words. Years ago, long before I was a pastor or a writer or a church leader, I was a young chicken farmer who led a Bible study of young people. During this time, I had become one of Bill's spiritual fathers.

Bill was now a spiritual father to those he had discipled in Barbados; and the Barbadian Christians who were now going to Africa and leading Gambians to Christ were a bit like my spiritual great grand-children. Generations to come would receive God's promises because a chicken farmer had been obedient to God's call to disciple a bunch of teenagers more than twenty years ago. Yes, this was part of my spiritual legacy. As I pondered this reality, I was deeply moved by the Lord. It was as if I was the recipient of a large inheritance!

A sweeping revival is just around the corner. God's people need to be alert to accommodate the great harvest this will bring into the king-dom of God. Spiritual parents will need to be ready to obey His call and take these young Christians under their wings. God has called you to be a spiritual parent. The Lord wants to give you a spiritual legacy. You may not feel ready, in fact, you may feel unprepared. Neverthe-less, God's call remains on your life.

Restoring the New Testament pattern

Although for the past 1700 years, much of the church of Jesus Christ has strayed from the truth of relational restoration between fa-thers and sons, the Lord is breathing a fresh word in our generation to His people. Rather than having the focus on meetings and buildings which promote *programs* to encourage the spiritual growth of believ-ers, He is calling us back to be His *family* and get back to the New Testament truth of building families. Many believers are meeting house to house in small groups throughout the world because the Lord is restoring this sense of family to the body of Christ. Christians are again beginning to relive the book of Acts. They are seeing the importance of empowering and parenting the next generation.

Parachurch organizations have understood this truth for years. Or-ganizations like the *Navigators, Campus Crusade For Christ,* and *Youth With a Mission* applied Ephesians 4:16 in their ministry operations and found that if everyone is trained, the body of Christ will expand and grow: "...the whole body, joined and knit together by what every joint supplies, according to the effective working by which every part does its share...." The body of Christ is meant to intricately fit together like the human body. When all members are working, the body of Christ will be healthy and grow.

Jesus wants His church to be restored to the New Testament pat-tern of family life. He ministered to the multitudes but focused on a few. These disciples changed the world! I believe we are living in the days of preparation and restoration. God is preparing us for the job He has for us to do. We are pressing on "to take hold of that for which Christ Jesus took hold of me [us]" (Philippians 3:12 NIV). As we press on and determine to follow the pattern Jesus has set before us, He promises times of refreshing and restoration: "Repent therefore...so that times of refreshing many come from the presence of the Lord...until the times of restoration of all things..." (Acts 3:19,21).

New wine for new wineskins

In the early 1970's, a group of young people (mostly 16-22 year olds) and myself started a friendship-evangelism ministry in our area. God laid a burden on our hearts for the unchurched youth in a neighboring community, and we were up for the challenge. We wanted to make a difference in the world we lived in and show the love of Jesus to those who rarely heard His name except in a profane utterance. Through one-on-one friendship evangelism utilizing clubs and coffeehouses, the fruits of our labor paid off. Many young people came to Christ.

Although we tried for a very long time to get these young people involved in our local churches, it just was not working. The existing churches were not flexible enough for these new Christians. Why? New Christians need new structures in which to grow. Jesus said, "And no one puts new wine into old wineskins; or else the new wine will burst the wineskins and be spilled, and the wineskins will be ruined. But new wine must be put into new wineskins, and both are preserved" (Luke 5:37-38). The new Christians were like new wine, still in the process of fermentation. When put in old wineskins (existing church structures), they were not compatible.

Of course, we did not know about the truth of new wine and new wineskins then. But God was faithful. We opened up our home to "father and mother" these kids, and soon young people were crowded in our living room every week. From these inauspicious beginnings, small groups were birthed. As we broke down into small groups to train these kids, we were preparing them for the next generation of believers. It was hard work and required commitment, but it was worth it to see them grow in God and reach others.

Today, I have the privilege of serving as the International Director of a worldwide family of churches that had its beginnings through this small group ministry.

Thirsting for new wine

I believe the Lord is preparing to pour out His Spirit and bring revival to the church in these last days. There will be a greater awakening to the things of God in our communities, and multiplied thousands will be drawn into the kingdom of God. When the Lord pours out this new wine, we must have the new wineskins prepared or we will lose the harvest. The new wineskins (church structures) of the early church were simplistic: people met from house to house.

Down through history, there are those who duplicated this working method of the early church with positive results. John Wesley, the founder of the Methodist church, set up thousands of "class meetings" where people met in homes to grow in God during the eighteenth and nineteenth centuries. He once made the comment, "More has happened in people's lives in close fellowship than in ten years of public preaching."

In the twentieth century, David Yonggi Cho from Korea, and now the pastor of the world's largest church in Seoul, also followed the New Testament's church's example of small groups. I believe our Lord's strategy to prepare for the harvest is still the same—He wants to use common ordinary believers who have encountered an extraordinary God to meet together as spiritual families from house to house to disciple and train, preparing for the harvest.

Many Christians today are thirsting for this great influx of new wine—new believers pouring into His kingdom. God is placing a desire within spiritual fathers and mothers to welcome these believers into the kingdom and then train them as spiritual sons and daughters. Small groups provide an ideal structure for this kind of training. The cell group is meant to be a spiritual family with the leaders and other spiritual moms and dads in the group taking responsibility to train the spiritual children. The purpose of a small group is to develop and produce mature Christians. When a young man and woman come together at the church altar to be married, there is an expectation that they will eventually have children. The same principle applies to spiritual families. When people are in love with Jesus and with each other, spiritual children are the result. The expectation, of course, is that these children will eventually grow up and reproduce on their own. Mature believers will parent spiritual children. Eventually the children grow up and start their own families.

Although cell groups, Bible study groups and other small groups are wonderful wineskins for spiritual parenting, the small groups in themselves are not the answer. In other words, it is not the structure itself that is significant, but the relationships occurring within its perimeters. If the people in the small groups do not practice spiritual parenting, they can find their groups quickly becoming as boring and as lifeless as any other structure. The life comes in the active father-son and mother-daughter relationships taking place within the group.

The need of the hour

Many churches are waking up to the need of the hour. They are providing small groups where relationships can be nurtured and people can grow spiritually. In the small groups, people pray together and focus on reaching others for Christ. The believers practice hospitality in their homes and know one another as real people. Each believer assumes the responsibility to help a younger Christian grow in his new life in Christ as they meet together for prayer, Bible study, and to discuss questions about life. Real spiritual parenting happens when believers are either being discipled or discipling others. This forces "consumers" or "former spectators" to become active spiritual parents.

In his book, *The Vanguard Leader*, Frank Damazio emphasizes this point, "Religious consumerism tempts the church to direct its energy to satisfy the expectations of members as if they were simply consumers. Rather, the church should focus its energy on accomplishing God's primary purpose: developing mature believers and reaching the world with the gospel." [1]

Every saint can parent

My friend Jim Pesce started a new church, Harvest Family Community Church, in Keswick, Ontario in 1996. Jim and his wife Deb are committed to practicing the principles of spiritual fathering and mothering. More than 84% of the members in their church are new believers who have come to Christ since their church started. Already they have ten cell (family) groups for spiritual parenting. Jim and Deb are dedicated to mentoring them so these "children" can go on to parent others. Their personal insights here show us how they started from the ground up to train new believers to be spiritual parents:

My wife Deb and I have discovered that it is those people we *fathered* that are the ones who go on with the Lord in devotion and ministry as we multiplied ourselves through them. So, at the start of our new church, Deb and I spent most of our time with about six newly saved couples. We not only ministered as a team but chose to spend free time together having fun. This is important. Most new Christians need more care and support than instruction.

We've also discovered that the ones we brought to Christ are the closest to us. They have our "spiritual DNA," they share our vision and our hearts and have our full trust. Because we are like family, there is much room for acceptance, correction, and patience to cover the many offenses we cause one another. They need to know that we will be with them over the long haul and accept them with all their flaws and sins. We love them for who they are, not for what they can accomplish for us.

We believe in them! Only by spending time with others can they "catch our spirit." Our passions become theirs as they walk with us in ministry situations.

The greatest struggle we face in fathering is choosing to say "no" to the many other demanding voices that would keep us from choosing to spend quality time with those special few we are fathering. Busyness is the destroyer of spiritual parenting.

In the last four years of mentoring ministry, we multiplied our cells, and today have 22 people capable of leading and growing cells. This shows the power of mentoring considering the fact that we started from scratch with almost all new Christians.

Just as their name contains it—Harvest Family Community Church is a spiritual *family* that consists of spiritual parents and children. They have discovered that every saint is called to parent as they grow to spiritual maturity.

Omar and Pat Beiler, serving for the past seven years as missionaries to Austria, are a couple that grew an existing church by mentoring several young people from the university in Vienna. This small Bible study group expanded as the Beilers became spiritual parents to the subsequent young believers. Four years after starting the small group ministry, they invited me to conduct a training seminar for them. I was amazed! They had 400 people attending 36 small spiritual family groups scattered throughout their city. There were 75 young leaders attending the seminar who were already producing spiritual children of their own. This church, that has focused on spiritual parenting, had become the largest free church in the history of the nation of Austria since the days of the Reformation, all within four years!

The timing of God for fathering

As long as the earth remains, Genesis 8:22 tells us, there will be seasons. Life is filled with seasons of time. I would never think to swim in a lake during our cold Pennsylvanian wintertime. It is simply the wrong season to do it. Likewise, in the summertime, my snow shovel is put away. I don't need it until the winter season.

Timing is paramount. Jesus worked in his father's carpentry shop until the *time appointed* by the heavenly Father for Him to begin His public ministry. Jesus infuriated the religious leaders of His day by His claims of deity, and they wanted to kill him immediately. But "...his *time had not yet come"* (John 7:30 NIV) and Jesus continued to preach until the *time* came for Him to leave this world (John 13:1). Abraham looked expectantly for a city designed and built by God, but lived in a tent like a mere visitor because the timing for God's promise was not right. Moses missed the timing of God by 40 years when he killed an Egyptian. But God gave him another chance, and the timing was right 40 years later when the Lord called him at the burning bush to lead his people out of bondage.

God's timing to becoming a spiritual parent is paramount. His time-table or schedule is much better than ours. He is much more concerned about the process than the end result. God sees a beautiful diamond in each one of us, but He has to cut out those impurities in our lives to make us sparkle (to look like Jesus). The junk in our lives must go before Jesus can shape us. Whatever the Lord can find in our lives that does not look like Jesus must go.

Becoming more like Jesus is a journey, not a destination. Over time and a sometimes bumpy road, we will see results. God will use us in our time of preparation. We need to make sure we have oil in our lamps like the ten virgins in Matthew 25. We need to be faithful to what God sets before us.

The Lord is patient with us during our preparation time. When I came to the Lord as an eighteen-year-old young man, I spent time memorizing scripture because I believed it would prepare me for a future time. As a young married couple, my wife and I were missionaries to needy people in South Carolina for one year. This time of preparation was invaluable as we learned to practice compassion and servanthood firsthand. Later, as a pastor of a church, I was being prepared even then for my present role as an overseer of a team of spiritual fathers and mothers who serve church leaders of an international family of churches scattered across five continents.

I love to hold my grandson in my arms and look into his tiny face gazing back at me. I am part of his biological inheritance, but what will his spiritual inheritance be? I believe he will experience that flow of generational blessing and inheritance from father to son. By God's grace, he will develop the heart of a father as his natural father and spiritual fathers take the time to mentor him spiritually. God's desire is for the heart of the fathers to turn toward the children. Only then will we see a rich inheritance handed down.

In the next chapter, let's look at some practical ways we can develop spiritual parenting relationships so we can pass on an enduring legacy and inheritance.

Notes
[1]   Frank Damazio, *The Vanguard Leader*, (Portland, Oregon: Bible Temple Publishing, 1994), p. 135.

CHAPTER 10

Let's Get Practical

Principles to help you build relationships

L es is on the pastoral team of one of our churches in Pennsylvania. He is eternally grateful to a man who encouraged him when he encountered Christ as a young adult: "My life was dramatically changed when I came to Christ, and I started attending a church, but a few months later, after attending every church meeting and activity I could find within the church walls, I still felt disconnected and insecure in my faith. Everyone else seemed to have it all together. Sure, I was learning a lot and had made many friends, but initially I had no one I really trusted to ask those soul-searching questions that nagged and threatened to destroy my newly found faith. I really was at a loss to know how to apply the truth of God's Word to my life.

"If it had not been for a 77-year-old spiritual father from my church who took a special interest in me, I would have probably thrown in the towel. But this elderly man patiently answered my searching questions as he sacrificially devoted hours explaining the scriptures to me. In addition, he spent time just being my friend. Through the mentoring of my first spiritual dad, I was firmly planted in God's Word and grew spiritually strong.

"I am convinced that this man and the subsequent spiritual fathers the Lord brought into my life were key factors in my maturing process in Christ. I clearly remember the night one of my spiritual fathers called me on the phone and asked me to go with him to pray for a sick man from our church. I had never done this before. As we walked into the man's home, my spiritual father handed me a bottle of oil so we could pray for him, anointing him with oil according to James, chapter 5. I opened the bottle, and dumped the whole bottle of oil on him. The poor guy had oil running down over his face onto his shoulders. I almost drowned him!

"On the way home that evening, my spiritual father gently advised me, 'Lester, next time, go a bit light on the oil!' He treated me like a son and loved me unconditionally even when I made mistakes. I learned by practical demonstration the importance of training others by example.

"These caring father-son relationships carried me through my first years as a Christian. My spiritual fathers 'passed the baton' to me, depositing in me a desire to be a father to others. I am so grateful."

Les determined he would take the biblical challenge to give his life to others and copy his spiritual fathers' examples. Today, Les is a pastor who challenges all believers to demonstrate the love of God in action by developing vital relationships with younger Christians, and in doing so, perpetuates a legacy of spiritual parenting.

Each one fathers one

By shadowing mentors in their daily lives, a spiritual son or daughter can learn the basics of spiritual fathering quickly and easily. It is the start of a powerful legacy to pass on. We have to remember that legacies come after the fact. If we dwell on the end results of spiritual fathering, we could get overwhelmed.

Spiritual fathering is a process, and sometimes a long one! But as "each one fathers one" our efforts are multiplied. The unique teaching methods of Dr. Frank Laubach give us an idea how this form of multiplication could work for spiritual fathering:

Dr. Frank Laubach's epitaph ascribes to him the following title: "The man who taught the world to read." Dr. Laubach popularized the phrase "each one teach one." Via his simple four-word strategy of teaching one person to read under the condition that each would teach another to read, several million people have now experienced the thrill and freedom of reading for the first time. The chain continues to this day, long after his death. Today the Laubach Method has more than eighty thousand volunteers worldwide.

Pause for sixty seconds and try to imagine the implications of this: You mentor 12, who mentor 12, equaling 144!
who mentor 12, equaling 1,728!
who mentor 12, equaling 20,736!
who mentor 12, equaling 248,832!
who mentor 12, equaling 2,985,984!
Is an unbroken chain of mentors realistic? Probably not! But the point is clear. Even if only a small fraction of protégés follow through by mentoring someone else, a significant difference will be made in the number of leaders in the next centuries—or until the Lord returns![1]

You can mentor and be mentored at the same time

The potential of spiritual parenting is phenomenal! Multiplication means *to grow and increase by number*, and that is exactly what happens. Quite naturally, in spiritual family relationships, spiritual babies grow into young men or women and finally become spiritual fathers or mothers themselves. And before you know it, a spiritual legacy is created. The phenomenal result of spiritual parenting is the multiplication that occurs. Why does it work so well? The process multiplies with exponential force because you do not have to wait until you are a spiritual giant in order to be a spiritual father or mother—you can mentor and be mentored at the same time. Since you can *have* a spiritual father and *be* a spiritual father simultaneously, spiritual fathers and mothers are constantly released.

Now that you know you are called to be a spiritual parent, how do you go about doing it? Let's begin by looking at our calling and three key principles of parenting that will help us along the way.

Know you are called

First of all, spiritual parenting is voluntary and intentional. You must want to do it because you feel God's specific call on your life to help people grow in Christ. You must be committed to their success. Being a spiritual mom or dad is not a duty; it is a privilege. Did you ever notice how many times Paul, the apostle, opened his letters with an expression of gratitude for those he fathered in the Lord? The epistle of Paul to Titus greets Titus: "my true son in our common faith" (Titus

1:4). He saw people as gifts from the Lord to cherish and encourage. They were not a burden but a reason to rejoice.

Total dependence on the Lord is a prerequisite for spiritual parenting. Psalm 127 says, "Unless the Lord builds the house, they labor in vain who build it." Unless we know we are called and depend fully on the Lord to guide us as spiritual parents, our work and effort is in vain. It is God who builds the lives of our spiritual children. We are only tools in His hands. This same Bible chapter goes on to say that sons are a heritage from the Lord, born in one's youth. I believe this means we can start early! We don't have to wait until we have it all together to train spiritual sons and daughters. No one is ever completely ready to be a parent but we will learn along the way.

Be available as the Lord leads

After you know you are called to be a spiritual father or mother, you have to intentionally go about your task—that of making yourself available. To invest our lives in another person, we must not be so busy that it becomes next to impossible. The desire to mentor a spiritual son or daughter needs to come out of a deep and passionate love relationship with Jesus that spills over into a willingness to make time to serve and love unconditionally.

Three keys to spiritual parenting principles

I believe there are three keys to open up the door of discovery to valuable spiritual parenting principles. In a nutshell, you could say your task as a spiritual parent is to "initiate, build and release." Parents must first find their spiritual children (*initiate* the relationship), then nurture and provide for them (*build* and encourage their lives) and lastly *release* them to do the same thing.

1. Initiate the relationship

Jesus *initiated* the relationships with His disciples, seeking twelve men out of seventy to be His key disciples. Whether you are a potential spiritual father or a son or both, the first place to begin a relationship is on your knees in prayer. Begin by praying that God will reveal to you the person you should mentor or who should mentor you. This person may be in a small group you attend, someone in your local church or at your workplace, or someone involved in ministry with you. Then dare to make the first move. The initiating of the relationship can go either way. The father can ask the son, or the son can ask the father. If it is God's will, He will put the relationship together in His timing.

The relationship must be mutual. The relationship, of course, must be mutual. There must be a sense on both sides that God is asking for a mutual investment in the relationship. Both parent and child must recognize their need for the relationship: "Can two walk together, unless they are agreed?" (Amos 3:3). When there is mutual faith for the relationship (Romans 14:23), we will be assured of its healthy existence because it will be God-ordained. If we believe we are called to a spiritual father-son relationship with someone and he does not feel the same way, we must lay it down. Perhaps the timing is wrong. The scriptures tell us we "know in part." Maybe we did not hear from God clearly.

Computer matching? Not necessarily! Peter Bunton from England, who serves both with YWAM and as the coordinator of DOVE International in Europe, has had years of experience in training and mentoring young people. He gives this advice about what to look for while initiating the relationship: "Often two people will be drawn together (often subconsciously) because of similar gifts and callings. However, a spiritual father or mother should be prepared to father or mother those of different personalities and gifts. Sometimes that very different person is needed to help spiritual sons or daughters learn other facets of their ministry. A test of a spiritual father's security is whether he can help someone more gifted than himself!"

I agree. It is a natural desire of parents to see greatness in their children—to make the world a better place! Likewise, a spiritual father should expect and desire his sons to go far beyond him spiritually. Whether the son already has many gifts or receives a new impartation from the father, it should be a spiritual father's greatest joy to see his children succeed.

Love: the pivotal point of the relationship. Regardless of their giftings, it is more important for the father and son to really enjoy and *like* being with each other than it is for them to be *alike* in giftings or personality. Look at the variety of leaders Jesus recruited.

I like how Gunter Krallman describes how and why Jesus recruited His followers: "As a leader Jesus knew that the success or failure of his mission would decisively depend on the selection of the right helpers. Thus he took the initiative in calling men to become disciples, a step as unprecedented in rabbinic tradition as the fact that he called them to follow not just his teaching but him as a person. Jesus did not merely recruit them for their intellectual benefit or for a task, he recruited them for a relationship." [2]

In other words, in addition to training them, Jesus also wanted to *fellowship* with them relationally. He loved them and enjoyed spending time with each one. He called the twelve that they *might be with Him* (Mark 3:14). Love will be the pivotal point on which a spiritual fathering relationship exists.

I also find it interesting to notice that although the word *disciple* is used 225 times in the gospels, Jesus only used it two times. Jesus preferred instead to use the word *friends.* More than wanting disciples or apprentices to train, Jesus wanted to be in relationship as a friend to the spiritual sons he was developing. He knew that you can impress people from a distance, but you can only affect their lives up close.

2. Build the relationship

In the course of Jesus' friendship with His disciples, He modeled practical spiritual fathering. For three and a half years, He focused on *building*—nurturing and preparing these twelve to fulfill the Lord's purpose for their lives. The disciples were His constant companions. From the mountains to the sea, from the temple gates to the Garden of Gethsemane, He modeled true fatherhood. Taking our cue from Jesus, after we find our spiritual son or daughter to mentor, we need to proactively *build* our relationship.

If the spiritual father does not already know his spiritual son very well, he will need to spend time with him. Getting to know someone takes intentional effort.

We may want to start out by spending time together doing something we both enjoy, like fishing or baking cookies. We could talk about where we came from, our current status, and our hopes and dreams for the future.

Discuss expectations. At the outset of the relationship, it is wise to discuss expectations. What are both sides looking for? How often will they meet? Is the relationship meant to be long-term or short-term? Are there already certain areas of life and ministry that the son or daughter needs to grow in? How often should the relationship be evaluated? Are there any major skeletons in the closet likely to come out? Be honest and open.

Create an atmosphere of trust and respect. The first step toward building a healthy relationship is to trust and respect each other. The son needs to be assured of his father's love for him. An atmosphere must be provided that allows him to be himself without fear of judgment or impatience on the father's part. I heard someone say once that God calls us to a higher form of love, a love that does not wait for people to change. Spiritual fathers and mothers will accept their sons and daughters as they are, even as they gently encourage them to grow.

It is caught more than taught. Spontaneous contact is important. Since mentoring is more caught than taught, informal interaction models the kingdom of God by showing how Christianity works in real life. In His everyday life, Jesus modeled the Christ-like character traits we need to emulate—compassion, wisdom, honesty, purity, etc. The people you are training need to see you in your everyday world and witness firsthand how you deal with life's situations. Open your home to them and let them observe your real-life family relationships and how you handle the situation when your teenager comes in past curfew. Invite them over for meals and make them feel a part of your family. Have them help you build storage shelves for your garage. Hang out together, golf together, shop together, eat together, fish together, bake together, weed the garden together, attend a sporting event together—as you spend time together, life issues will surface to discuss and learn from as we aim for Christ-likeness.

On-the-job training. The goal of spiritual parenting is to increase their children's effectiveness in the kingdom. If you are training someone for ministry, take them along to the hospital when you visit a sick member from your small group. Participate with them in an evangelism outreach to your community. Ask for their input in these ministry situations. What would they do differently if they were you? What are their observations? How can these observations be turned into ministry principles? This on-the-job training allows them to see and learn firsthand. Mistakes will be made. You can count on it. But remember, God is a God of second chances. If Jonah could receive a second chance, so can we!

Delegate assignments to the spiritual son or daughter after they have seen you do it. If there is a need for someone to be baptized in water, don't just do it yourself. Take your son along with you into the water. Then the next time there is a need for water baptism, you both go in the water, but this time, your son leads and you help him. And finally, the next time he can be responsible for the baptism himself and take along *his* spiritual son. Get the picture? Start with small things and increase to greater responsibilities.

As we observe our spiritual sons or daughters in their own ministry situations, it is important to evaluate them and give feedback, including areas for suggested growth and improvement. New leaders need to be allowed to lead and make their own mistakes. Listen to your spiritual son or daughter tell you about the "new," successful idea that you have used a dozen times. Help them analyze "why" if they have failed. Encourage them to press on. Share with them the feelings of fear and inadequacy you have felt many times. Be vulnerable. This shows that you are interested in them as people.

3. Finally, release them!

After Jesus rose from the dead and just before He ascended into heaven, He encouraged the twelve to take on the responsibility of His church. By taking this action, Jesus set the example for us to release our spiritual sons to "go and do it." We need not be afraid of this step. We will know when it is time. Remember, the heart of spiritual fathering is to develop leaders, and a spiritual father will know when they are ready to go out on their own. They are ready to fly out of the nest, so to speak, because we believe in them and have confidence in them. As spiritual parents, we have helped them discover and develop their gifts, and they are now controlled and energized by the Holy Spirit. They are prepared and equipped to parent the next generation.

Jesus sent out the seventy in Luke chapter 10 "to go and do it"! When they returned He exclaimed, "I saw Satan fall like lightning from heaven." Jesus witnessed the fact that His ministry was multiplied by seventy times, and it had confounded the work of the enemy. As I mentioned before, Jesus promises that we will do greater works than He did because He has gone to the Father (John 14:12).

What are the greater works? Part of the answer is the multiplication of the ministry of Jesus through each of His spiritual children. And He calls us to do the same! He wants us to experience the joy of multiplication of His ministry as we become spiritual parents to those whom the Lord has called us.

We must release them to reproduce!

While in Hawaii teaching a leadership-training seminar at Grace Bible Church in Honolulu, I met Norman Nakanishi. He had been sent out of this church a year before to plant a new church in neighboring Pearl City. This church plant had reached many young people with the gospel within the past two years, and seventy young people had given their lives to Christ within the past few weeks. I wanted to experience this dynamic ministry for myself, so Norman agreed to take me to a youth meeting before he dropped me off at the airport.

We jumped into Norman's station wagon and headed for the local school where the meeting was held. Inside the school, the lights were off except for the stage lights and the young people were singing wholeheartedly, worshiping the Lord with their arms outstretched. They meant business with God! After a time of worship, everyone sat down and the lights flicked on. The youth pastor grabbed the microphone, "Everyone needs to be in a power huddle," he charged the group of new believers. "It is a place where you can get to know other kids. There are people to help you out when you have a problem or a question about your life with God."

After the meeting, Norman explained the truth they discovered recently, "We are touching 225 young people, mostly from unsaved homes. We have found that these kids need relationships. So we started power huddles—cell groups for young people. We have found that the young people in power huddles are growing in God, while the young people that are not getting involved are having a hard time."

With the heart of a spiritual parent, Norman revealed his strategy: "I've already explained to the church that I told our youth pastor he could plant a new church with these young people whenever he believes the time is right. I had to verbalize this, or else I might revert to keeping him here in order to help me build this church."

Norman had learned the value of reaching the next generation and trusting them to reproduce themselves. There is a whole new generation of pastors, cell group leaders and church planters among us. They are enthusiastic and often unconventional. Though we parents may not always understand, we must always encourage them to dream big and allow God to use us to help them fulfill those dreams.

Empower the next generation

If you are a pastor or a Christian leader, let me take a moment and speak with you. We must commission this next generation to establish their own power huddles and their own new churches. We must not hold them back. Let's empower these young people. And then rejoice with them when they reproduce!

Many of the younger generation in our churches are sensing a desire to experience something new. They are no longer satisfied with the church structure in which they have lived. We need to release them to build their own homes and reproduce. A few years ago Rick Joyner from Charlotte, North Carolina, told a group of pastors in our city: "Pastors sometimes don't like having young stallions in their churches. They seem to cause too many problems. But only young stallions can reproduce. Resist the temptation to "fix" them so they cannot reproduce!"

A group of 18 to 35 year olds recently shared with me: "We like our churches and our pastors, but our present churches are not something we want to give our lives for. We lead cell groups, youth groups and serve in the church, but we do not want to do this our whole lives. God is calling us to something new—new kinds of churches. We are not even sure what it will look like, but we want the opportunity to try. We are not rebellious. We want the blessing of the leaders of our churches. We respect and honor them. But we want to build our own house. There are things the Lord has placed inside of us that we desire to see become reality. It is good to have a room within our father's house, but we have a God-given desire to build a new home."

I understood completely. I remembered how I felt when I was in my 20's and the Lord called me to start a new church—a new wineskin. However, new wineskins eventually get old, and my generation of stallions are now the parents. We find that God has placed the same burden in the younger generation to birth new wineskins, but they have a different vision for a different era and a different generation. They come into the kingdom looking for reality—not religious structures. They want relationships—not outdated church programs.

Now that we've learned the three keys to spiritual parenting relationships: initiating, building and releasing, we can move on to the practical "how to's" of building the relationship. In the next chapter, we'll give you some tips for healthy spiritual parenting relationships.

Notes

[1]   Bobb Biehl, *Mentoring,* (Nashville, Tennessee: Broadman & Holman Publishers, 1996), p. 179.
[2]   Gunter Krallman, *Mentoring For Mission,* (Hong Kong: Jensco Ltd., 1992), p.50.

CHAPTER 11

How Does It Really Work?

The "how to's" of spiritual fathering and mothering

Spiritual parents are partners in helping their children discover what God intends for them. They will do all they can to help them reach that goal. George MacDonald once said, "If I can put one touch of rosy sunset into the life of any man or woman, I shall feel that I have worked with God."

How can we practically "work with God" to cultivate spiritual fathering that will develop into trusted and honest relationships? Let's get down into the nuts and bolts of the relationship and take a look at how the Lord wants us to build healthy spiritual relationships.

Pray, pray, pray

For the success of the spiritual parenting relationship, prayer needs to be woven into its very fabric. Praying for our spiritual son or daughter will wrap them in the Lord's protection. Paul says in Galatians 4:19 that he "labors in the pains of childbirth" for the Galatian church until Christ is formed in them. He invested a lot of time in these Christians whom he affectionately calls his "children," and he is expecting that each one will grow up spiritually strong. Much of his "labor" was in prayer for the Galatians.

Ibrahim Omondi, who pastors DOVE Christian Fellowship in Nairobi, Kenya, and serves as a spiritual father to other church leaders in East Africa, describes how prayer with a spiritual father brought him to a place of spiritual maturity: "Those who had discipled me as a young Christian had long moved out of my life... I was left on my own until, at a Bible School, I met an elderly professor who asked if I could pray with him regularly. Our weekly prayer meetings soon took on the form of a father-son relationship. I loved it. For once I recognized what I had missed throughout my Christian walk. I was able to open up in prayer. The deepest secrets of my life found no hiding place. I felt a new sense of security, love and deep humility."

Job rose early every morning and offered a sacrifice for each of his children (Job 1:5). Jesus is at the right hand of the Father right now interceding, not only for the world in general but for us individually (Romans 8:34). We must pray specific prayers for our spiritual children. Pray that they will run to God and hunger for God's Word. Pray that they will learn to resist temptation and flee from it.

Lifetime or short-term commitment?

Is availability in a spiritual fathering relationship a lifetime commitment? It may or may not be. Discuss, early on, if you foresee the relationship to be for a certain period of time or if it is meant to continue in an ongoing long-term relationship (of course, this needs to be evaluated and updated periodically). A spiritual parent may maintain a close relationship for a lifetime with a spiritual child, but with others the relationship may be a close one for only a few years or even months. Whether it is for a predetermined period of time or an ongoing commitment, it is the relationship that is vital! Keep it healthy by periodically examining the relationship to determine if continuing it is God's best plan.

Eventually, a spiritual father and his son may determine the son can make it on his own with less input from the father. In a natural family, when a child marries, he is still your son. You may no longer have as much input in his life, but he remains a son. In some relationships, a phone call now and then will be all it takes to maintain a father-son relationship. It is important that a son or daughter knows his father or mother is available if needed.

Be transparent and vulnerable

Spiritual fathering involves a sense of vulnerability and willingness to open our lives to one another. It is encouraging and accepting another person without reservation. A spiritual father will not be afraid to take the risk to share his life openly with another. Transparency leads to intimacy. If a father is free to reveal his true feelings, his son learns to open up too. Spiritual fathers do not hesitate to talk about their failures as well as their successes. People identify with you when they see your weaknesses because you are willing to say, "Follow me as I, a sinful human being, follow Christ."

Early in our marriage, LaVerne and I went to see a marriage counselor. Being open about this area of our lives has encouraged many married couples to get the help they have needed when facing a crisis in their marriage.

When we are transparent, a spiritual son or daughter doesn't have to feel alone in their struggles, neither will they be tempted to put their spiritual father or mother up on a pedestal. Spiritual sons or daughters will not think less of their spiritual parents when they know their struggles—they will probably just be relieved that they are normal!

Jane, a young married woman describes the relief she felt when "the giant of a spiritual woman" she looked to as a mentor revealed that even her 30-year-old marriage experienced "bumps in the road" when she and her husband did not see eye to eye. "Just hearing her admit to her unspiritual thoughts helped me to see that she was learning to live in the grace of God in her marriage too, and I was not alone in my problems," said Jane.

Jane was encouraged because her spiritual mother dared to say, "I am committed to Jesus Christ, and I'm going to be honest with you about how consistently I live my Christian life."

Point them to Jesus

The truth of Galatians 4:2, that children need guardians and stewards, also applies to our spiritual sons or daughters. Looking out for them, however, does not mean we stand guard duty. We don't peer over their shoulders waiting for them to make a wrong move. If they do need correction, the way we approach the issue is as important as what we say. Spiritual fathering is not a way to get people to do what we want them to do or for them to serve our ambitions. Instead, we must help them discern God's will for their lives while holding them accountable to do it.

What is accountability? Personal accountability is finding out from God what He wants us to do and then asking someone to hold us accountable to do those things. It is helpful to check up on each other so we stay on a safe path. If a spiritual daughter wants to be held accountable to her spiritual mother for a certain area in her life that needs support, it does not mean the mother tells her what to do. Remember, we are only *pointing* to Jesus; people need to make their own decisions.

Normally a father-son relationship is one of deep friendship and trust, so if a son seems to be making an unwise decision or is participating in a destructive behavior, a father that expresses his concerns will be heard. Fathers should not condemn but instead confront their son or daughter lovingly. In this way, he or she will be teachable and open to input.

Learn to ask vital questions

Mentoring with accountability is done with patience and love. Ask questions to spur your sons or daughters on to new spiritual heights:
"How is your relationship with Jesus?"
"How is your relationship with your spouse?"
"Whom are you praying for?"
"Has your thought life been pure?"
"What sin has tempted you this week?"
"What struggles are you having in your life?"
"In what ways have you stepped out in faith lately?"
"Have you shared your faith this week?"
"Are you serving others in love?"
"What was your greatest joy this week?"
"What was your biggest disappointment?"
"What do you see yourself doing 5 or 10 years in the future?"
"How can I help you fulfill what the Lord has called you to do?"
Ask about their relationship with their spouse (if married) and children, or with their parents. Ask about their relationship with their church. Questions similar to these will motivate your sons and daughters and help them to be more like Christ. Of course, you will not bombard your spiritual sons or daughters with all these questions at one time! Additionally, it is not wise to preach at your spiritual children by using these types of questions as a leverage. Look for ways for these kinds of personal issues to naturally come up in your conversations over a period of time as the friendship develops.

How often?

Decide on some practical get-together times for the relationship. How often and how long should you meet? The answer to this question will vary. You may want to set up regular times to meet and communicate. One breakfast meeting each month may be adequate for a healthy relationship. New Christians may need more (weekly or bi-weekly). Meet both on your turf and on theirs. These planned, regular contacts should be interlaced with a lot of spontaneous contact.

Don't think you have to solve every problem

Because of the powerful connection of a spiritual parenting relationship, there is a danger of the parents taking on too much responsibility for the growth of the children. A son or daughter may grow dependent and begin to demand more than a father or mother can give. Before they know it, the relationship becomes self-serving.

In spiritual mothering relationships, women especially, with their need to form close friendships, may tend to absorb themselves too deeply in a relationship. If a relationship becomes possessive and demanding, it may be moving toward an unhealthy dependency.

Tony Fitzgerald from Church of the Nations has served as a spiritual father to church leaders scattered across the globe for more than twenty years. He recently gave this wise advice in one of our conversations, "Fathering is not to meet every need, but to be sure every need is met."

In the story of the Good Samaritan, the compassionate Samaritan attended to the wounded man's bruises, placed him on his donkey and took him to an inn. At that point, the Samaritan's job was finished. He left and entrusted the wounded man to the innkeeper. He did not meet every need of the wounded man, but made sure his every need was attended to.

Sometimes, spiritual fathers are available to help their sons meet certain needs, and then entrust them to others to meet further needs. When a spiritual father directs his son to helpful resources such as books, tapes, videos and other spiritual leaders and counselors, he is helping meet a need without directly meeting it himself.

Maintain proper boundaries

A relationship goes downhill when two people lean too much on each other rather than the Lord. If spiritual sons or daughters look to fathers or mothers to solve their problems or meet all their needs, the relationship becomes "need" driven.

"Dependent relationships become ingrown and create a seedbed for one person to become emotionally dependent on another," according to counselor Steve Prokopchak. In his book *Recognizing Emotional Dependency,* emotional dependency is defined as *the condition resulting when the ongoing presence and/or nurturing of another is believed necessary for personal security.* Steve goes on to say, "It's true that we need others. I believe that relationship with God and with others is the most important thing in life...However, our need for relationship cannot be allowed to become the center of a person's life. The emotionally dependent person feels as though he cannot exist or function without this relationship. Mistakenly, this association is an attempt to meet the need for intimacy and security."[1]

In spiritual parenting relationships, we must maintain proper boundaries in order to maintain healthy relationships. This means we must be sure of our identity in Christ and want to please Him rather than another person.

What if you need help?

You should be aware that sometimes you will need help to solve a severe problem in a son or daughter's life. You should not be alarmed by these situations. Whenever you have people progressing on a spiritual journey, you have some besetting sins that need to be dealt with. Stubborn struggles like this could involve depression, addictions to sex, alcohol, drugs, etc.

If your spiritual son or daughter has a severe, ongoing addiction that you are not prepared to deal with, discern if they would benefit from meeting with someone trained in setting people free through deliverance from demonic oppression or perhaps seeing a professional counselor. You can stay involved in the son or daughter's life and at the same time have the additional support available to help them through the difficult times.

Make it easy to get out of the relationship

There may come a time in a mentoring relationship that negative interpersonal dynamics make it impossible to continue on. When a once supportive relationship becomes critical and disappointment sets in, don't immediately bolt from the scene! First, address the root of the conflict—be candid and communicate and pray together. Try to resolve it as painlessly as possible. It may be helpful to have a trusted third party to guide you and your spiritual son (or father) through the conflict in the spiritual parenting relationship.

If it cannot be resolved, remember that a mentoring relationship is not a covenant bond; it is a spiritual impartation into the life of another that allows freedom and flexibility. If the time comes for a separation in the relationship, the love relationship we have with Christ and each other will help us discern how to graciously and lovingly bow out. Allow the Lord to be your comfort so you do not grow bitter or refuse to take the risk of another relationship.

Learn to empower those whom you mentor

Servanthood must be the crux of the parenting relationship. Servanthood releases sons and daughters to be all they can be, giving them power. I like the way Tom Marshall says it in *Understanding Leadership*: "A servant leader is willing to share power with others so that they are empowered, that is, they become freer, more autonomous, more capable and therefore more powerful."[2] A servant leader knows that the more people there are that have authority, the more authority there is to spread around. When the relationship centers on servanthood, it will rarely become selfish because it gives people the freedom to use their own gifts and abilities.

Multiple spiritual fathers

God often uses more than one spiritual father or mother in a person's life according to varying areas of need. For example, a spiritual father could mentor someone specifically in the areas of healthy family relationships. Another mentor could share his expertise in the area of financial management and budgeting. My natural father has served as a mentor to me for years in learning principles of sound financial management.

Yet another spiritual father or mother may mentor the same spiritual son or daughter in the area of Christian ministry. Yes, even ministry leaders need spiritual moms and dads. A pastor's wife needs to be mentored by another spiritually mature woman (preferably another pastor's wife who understands the needs of someone in leadership). In spiritual fathering, the buck does not stop at any point in the family hierarchy. A senior pastor of a church needs a spiritual father, too. This mentor could mentor him in sound decision-making principles in leadership, for example. I have various spiritual fathers in my life that I look to for spiritual advice and continual leadership development. I need these fathers in my life.

Spheres of spiritual fathering relationships

Along with the option of having more than one spiritual father or mother speaking into a spiritual son or daughter's life is the likely possibility that each relationship will be of varying levels of friendship and intimacy. It helps to understand the several spheres of relationships that Jesus had and apply this principle to spiritual parenting. Jesus had an inner circle of friends, namely, Peter, James and John. He spent quality time with these three, and John in particular. Jesus also closely mentored the twelve disciples with whom He traveled day to day. In addition, He was in relationship with the 70 disciples He sent out "...two by two ahead of him to every town and place where he was about to go" (Luke 10:1 NIV). Lastly, Jesus was a spiritual father to the 120 faithful believers that waited in the Upper Room for the promised Holy Spirit.

As a young leader, I felt I needed to be everyone's friend on an equal basis. I soon found there was not enough of me to go around! As I prayed and pondered Jesus' relationships with His disciples, it became clear to me that Jesus had to work with the same constraints we do. He clearly heard from His heavenly Father regarding which of the disciples He needed to spend most of His time with. It did not depend on how long He knew them or on their expectations. Jesus gave us the model to value all people, but even He could only develop close, deep friendships with some. Jesus did that which He knew His Father was leading Him to do concerning relationships (John 5:19).

Fathering new believers

If a spiritual son or daughter is a new Christian, you will want to disciple this young Christian—spend time studying the Bible together, answering questions, and praying together. The first few years after our cell-based church started, we discovered the pressing need for a basic biblical foundation course to help spiritual moms and dads parent new believers. So I wrote a twelve booklet series on basic Christian foundations that could be taught systematically from the scriptures. They are geared especially for spiritual parenting relationships, complete with teaching outlines and questions broken down into increments of time.[3] The response we got from these Christian doctrine booklets was amazing. Within a few short years over 100,000 of the booklets were distributed throughout the body of Christ. God's people are hungry for practical discipling tools to use in spiritual fathering and mothering relationships. Any biblical foundations series like this is an excellent tool to use in a spiritual parenting relationship for younger Christians because they have the specific need of getting grounded in God's Word.

Homogeneous fathering

Young mothers need older mothers to mentor them in areas of motherhood. Older professional women can mentor younger professional women. Businessmen benefit from having other businessmen mentor them in sound business practices. Widows who lost spouses years ago could mentor more recent widows. The term *homogeneous* refers to these "like" kinds of mentoring relationships that can be greatly beneficial.

Nelson Martin, a pastor who serves on the leadership team of DOVE Christian Fellowship International, heads up a "24 Hour Prayer Watch" for our family of churches. The prayer watch includes *prayer generals* who oversee *prayer warriors* who pray for the DCFI family around the clock. Some prayer generals mentor their prayer warriors to pray and hear from God, connecting them in a prayer mentoring relationship.

Couples can play a vital role in mentoring other couples in their marriage relationship. We have seen gratifying results with a successful couple-to-couple marriage mentoring program we utilize. The program, using the workbook *Called Together,* written by Steve and Mary Prokopchak, is a unique mentoring program designed for counselor mentors to equip engaged couples for marriage and beyond. The material teaches mature couples how to mentor others through varying phases of married life.[4]

Bruce Heckman, who oversees DOVE Mission International, has spent the past twenty years ministering in Muslim nations. He told me that he has come to the conclusion that one of the most effective ways to train missionaries is for an experienced missionary to mentor (become a spiritual father to) a younger more inexperienced missionary.

Men mentor men, women mentor women

While we are talking about "like" spiritual fathering and mothering relationships, it should be mentioned that we believe men should mentor men and women mentor women as modeled in Titus 2. "...that the older men be sober, reverent, sound in faith...likewise exhort the young men to be sober-minded...the older women likewise, that they be reverent in behavior...teachers of good things—that they admonish the young women to love their husbands...."

In counsel and example, the early Christian church followed the mentoring method of older women with younger women and older men with younger men.

There is a good reason for this. Fathering and mothering relationships fast become intimate friendships. Maintaining the boundaries of friendship between a man and a woman can be tricky. The deeply shared Christian love can be misinterpreted, leading to inappropriate emotional and physical attachments.

In my opinion, simply avoiding this trap is the best policy. "Abstain from all appearance of evil" says I Thessalonians 5:22 (KJV), or in my paraphrase, "stay as far away from the cliff as possible, so if you fall, you will not be devastated."

I believe it is entirely appropriate, however, for a husband and wife team to mentor a spiritual son or daughter together. In Acts 18:24-26, a husband and wife team, Aquila and Priscilla helped enlighten Apollos concerning his knowledge of the gospel. Aquila and Priscilla "took him aside and explained the way of God more accurately" to him (v. 26).

Individual and group mentoring

Some spiritual fathers will maintain a one-on-one mentoring relationship with a spiritual son and also mentor him in a small group setting where he meets with a group of sons to pray and study the Bible together. It is beneficial for spiritual children to have healthy interaction in a group setting with others while a spiritual parent observes and trains them. A group setting however, cannot take the place of a person-to-person relationship that occurs when a father sits down with his son eyeball-to-eyeball and intentionally takes the time to listen and really sense what he is feeling.

Bless your spiritual parents

Although the spiritual father or mother is mature enough to give freely without a thought of return, I think it is a good idea for a son or daughter to look for ways to bless his or her spiritual parent. Parents need encouragement too! Occasionally, they need to hear the actual words that they are having an impact on the lives of those they are mentoring. Words and actions of blessing are powerful. Spiritual children can bless their parents by sending cards of appreciation, spontaneous gifts or telling them by communicating words of encouragement face-to-face.

I firmly believe the following biblical promise to natural children also applies to spiritual children: "Honor your father and mother, which is the first commandment with promise: that it may be well with you and you may live long on the earth" (Ephesians 6:2-3).

Your children will grow up, and changes will occur

As spiritual parents encourage their spiritual children to grow up and have their own spiritual children, the relationship changes. Now spiritual parents talk to their son or daughter about their own parenting experiences. Spiritual parents will continue to parent their grown-up spiritual children as long as they need the input. In some ways, the children eventually become peers although they will always honor their parents. When children are babies, their parents meet all of their needs. When parents are elderly, the children often assume a role of responsibility for the well-being of the parents. Be aware of the possibilities of these potential changes in spiritual parenting relationships.

Hand over the ministry to those you are training

Do you remember the last principle of spiritual parenting from the previous chapter? *Release them* to go and do it themselves! I can't stress this enough. Keep handing the ministry over to those you are training with this mentoring-style leadership. The Levites were instructed to serve in the tent of meeting from age twenty-five through age fifty. At fifty years of age they were required to retire (Numbers 8:23-26) to serve the next generation of priests. They were called to pass on the ministry to those they were fathering.

Allow your spiritual sons and daughters to try new things for the first time and succeed. This is how the Ephesians 4:12 ministry of "equipping the saints for the work of ministry" is supposed to work. This kind of apprenticeship-modeling-discipleship-rolled-up-in-one is how you train leaders!

Remember, this works best within the context of a working New Testament style church where everyone gets the chance to participate through some type of effective cell group ministry. We all have the same opportunity to be spiritual fathers and mothers and train the next generation. The opportunities are limitless as we get trained from the ground up in cell groups. As we will learn in the next chapter, this kind of training helps us to develop into diverse kinds of fathers and mothers.

Notes

[1] Steve Prokopchak, *Recognizing Emotional Dependency*, (Ephrata, Pennsylvania: House to House Publications), p.8.

[2] Tom Marshall, *Understanding Leadership,* (Chichester, England: Sovereign World, 1991). p. 73.

[3] Larry Kreider, *Biblical Foundation Series*, (Ephrata, Pennsylvania: House to House Publications).

[4] Steve and Mary Prokopchak, *Called Together*, (Camp Hill, Pennsylvania: Horizon Books), 1999.

CHAPTER 12

Different Kinds of Fathers

How spiritual fathers and mothers
are trained from the ground up

B y this chapter, we see that spiritual families are best developed in settings where a powerful flow of ministry can occur as fathers pass on their spiritual impartation to their sons. These family settings or small "cells," initially foster relationships that can be grown naturally and powerfully because people realize they are ministers and can be grown into spiritual fathers or mothers as they carry out the work of ministry. My two decades of experience with small group ministry has convinced me that each member must learn how to pass on a spiritual impartation so that a legacy of spiritual families can continue.

If we do not develop believers in this way, we are failing to provide for a future and will lose our children. In his book *You Have Not Many Fathers*, Dr. Mark Hanby explains what happens all too frequently when the church refuses to recognize that the flow of power in the kingdom of God is through relationship with one another:

> Without the spiritual relationship of father to son, there can never be the passing of double portions or a true basis of spiritual authority and identity...The flow of all power in the kingdom of God is through relationship with one another. The amputation of relationship has left the church handicapped in power. The disjointed connection in the order of God's people has made some members lame and withered in spiritual atrophy. Other members have become exhausted, overburdened

with an unbalanced share of kingdom responsibility and care. To manifest a complete Christ to the whole world, spiritual connections must be restored and the balance of power shared by each member.[1]

I agree wholeheartedly! I believe the "balance of power can be shared" as spiritual impartations are passed on practically and easily from fathers to sons as they are trained in the spiritual "boot camp" of small groups. Many times these spiritual fathers and mothers move on to further leadership in the church. The easiest way to explain how a spiritual impartation is passed on is to give you a working example from our cell-based church.

Trained from the ground up

I had the privilege of serving as the pastor of a cell-based church in Pennsylvania for many years. By cell-based, I mean, everyone committed to the church is committed to other believers in a cell group, along with the cell leader. The cell leaders look to the leadership of their church as spiritual parents who give them guidance and provide vision for the whole church. We use the term *cell group* because of cells in our body that grow and eventually go through the process of mitosis, where one cell becomes two, two become four, and the process of multiplication continues. This process of cell multiplication was modeled in the book of Acts as the New Testament church met in homes in every city (Acts 20:20).

It all started in the late 1970's, when LaVerne and I found ourselves becoming spiritual parents to a group of young Christians, and we started a cell group in our home. By 1980, we had multiplied into two cell groups in two different homes. In October 1980, there were three cell groups and we started a new church, a Sunday morning "celebration" of about 25 people. By the grace of God, these cell groups continued to grow as people throughout our community came to Christ and many joined a spiritual family (cell) and our new church. Ten years later, in 1990, there were more than 2,300 people committed to our church in more than 125 cell groups. Churches were planted in Scotland, Brazil, and Kenya. (If you desire to read more about our story, you will find it in a book I wrote about our church's adventure in cell groups entitled *House to House).*[2]

In the process of our church growing and multiplying, hundreds of spiritual fathers and mothers were released as ministers to God's people through the cell groups. Here is one "boot camp" story of Carl Good's initial training and then imparting and passing on an inheritance as a spiritual father.

Carl was in his early 50's when he and his wife, Doris, from the small town of Manheim, Pennsylvania, started attending our church and participating in its cell ministry. An unassuming, quiet member of his cell group, Carl worked at a feed manufacturing plant. Doris was a buying agent for a local firm.

Cell leader. After a time, Carl and Doris' willingness to serve and be committed to relationships with people in their cell group caught the attention of their cell leaders. They were asked to consider leading a cell. With fear and trembling, they agreed to this new venture and completed our church's cell leader training course. After a few months as assistant cell leaders, Carl and Doris assumed leadership responsibility for their cell. They were not flashy, but they loved people, and their living room soon filled to capacity. They were a "do what you can, with what you have, where you are" kind of couple. People were naturally drawn to them because they were authentic. In time, they mentored assistant leaders in the group, raising up enough leaders to start another cell. Before long, they had launched two more cells, then three and four. Over the next few years, their cells continually grew and multiplied.

Local pastor. Meanwhile our church family was rapidly expanding, and we needed to add more support pastors to our staff who could "father" the cell leaders. As we prayed and looked for spiritual fathers among the cells, our eyes fell on Carl, a true pastor. He already was fathering the cell leaders. He had been trained in the seminary and boot camp of the cell group. Carl joined our paid staff and continued to be a "father" to the cell leaders in the greater Manheim area.

A few years later, the Lord called our church family to decentralize and plant eight autonomous new cell churches in our region, all at the same time. Who became the Senior Pastor (we use the term *senior elder*) of the new church in Manheim? You guessed it — Carl. Under Carl's leadership, this new Manheim cell church soon started a new cell group in the nation of Scotland. A Scottish couple, Duncan and

Kath, attending our cell-based *Church Planting and Leadership School,* joined a cell in the Manheim church. They returned to Scotland to plant a new cell, and it grew and multiplied to evolve into a new cell church. Duncan looks across the ocean to Carl as a spiritual father. The cell church in Manheim continues to start cells all over the community. They also planted two other new cell churches in Pennsylvania.

Apostolic leader. Carl turned 65 recently. He received much of his church leadership training in the local church, starting in his first cell group. His story has been, and remains, amazing to watch. Not too long ago, Carl turned the leadership of this church over to one of his capable elders whom he has fathered over the past few years. He now serves church leaders as a father. Today, various church leaders throughout our nation and the world look to Carl as their spiritual father. He serves on the DOVE Christian Fellowship International "Apostolic Council," which oversees leaders of more than 70 cell-based churches scattered across five continents. A few months ago, a leader in the body of Christ from another part of the United States told me, "I have been looking for a spiritual father all of my Christian life, and God has answered my prayers. Carl has become a father to me."

Carl worked in a feed manufacturing plant when the Lord called him to learn how to be a spiritual father. The Lord used Carl's experience of cell leader servanthood to prepare him for future service in His kingdom. Carl did not aspire to pastor a church, much less to pastor other pastors. He just loved Jesus and wanted to serve in a supportive role in the local church. But God had other plans—divine plans.

Carl was trained in the small group and moved on through the various kinds of spiritual fatherhood. First, he became a grassroots spiritual father who fathered new believers in Christ through the cell groups meeting from house to house (Romans 16:3-11).

Later, after multiplying his cell group various times, he became a pastor who focused his time on fathering cell group leaders meeting from city to city (Titus 1:5). He had now become a type of spiritual grandfather or church leader.

Still later, Carl became the "apostolic father" that he is today. He began to oversee and father leaders (pastors) of churches just as Paul, Barnabas, Aquila, Priscilla, Titus, Timothy and many more did in the early church. He entered the role of a spiritual great-grandfather!

We are all called to spiritual parenting

I should clarify that Carl's story is unique to Carl. Not everyone trained in the small group will become an apostolic father, a local pastor, or even a small group leader. But since every believer has a commission to lead new Christians into saving faith, we are all called to be spiritual fathers and mothers, whether we "birth" them to Christ or take them under our wing to mentor them.

Some small group leaders will remain small group leaders and impart their legacy within their group by training more small group leaders, because this is their call from God. They still become spiritual fathers and grandfathers because eventually, those whom they father in the Lord will become spiritual fathers to another generation. The lineage goes on and on.

Perhaps some of these small group leaders will develop into a pastor of a local church or an apostolic leader, but not all. We need to follow God's call on our lives, and not be pushed into a role of leadership that does not fit us! David tried on Saul's armor, but it did not fit. We cannot wear someone else's "armor."

Just remember, whether in an actual leadership level or not, every believer is called to some kind of spiritual parenting. In addition, we are all called to be fathered by those over us in the Lord who will bring loving training and protection to us. These relationships must be built by the Lord Himself, through His Holy Spirit.

Grassroots fathers—God's call for all of us!

The New Testament church was a grassroots movement meeting from house to house where ordinary people led others to Christ, lovingly fathered these new believers in Paul-Timothy-type relationships, and opened up their homes, generously serving each other. They shared their friendship with Jesus—extending His grace and forgiveness to the world. In these small group settings, they built loving relationships with one another and learned from the ground up how to become fathers. I like to call the kind of spiritual fathers and mothers trained in this setting *grassroots fathers.*

When our church started, we were a fledgling cell-based movement that started to grow by developing grassroots fathers. In the late 1970's, the Lord spoke to me asking if I would be willing to "be involved in the underground church." At the time, I knew little about cell groups and how the family-type relationships built there could impact our lives. But I got a picture of an underground church in the form of a tree: its trunk, branches and leaves are only half of the picture. The unnoticed half, the underground root system, nourishes the whole tree and keeps it healthy. The underground church is the believers gathered together in small groups to pray, evangelize and build healthy relationships with each other. These mutually accountable father-son, mother-daughter relationships are a vital connection for each member to experience spiritual growth, encouragement and reproduction.

We encouraged the believers at our church that each one could develop into a spiritual father or mother at the grassroots level. A grassroots father was a believer who was involved in discipling new believers, and in some cases, was also a cell leader or assistant leader in a small group setting, who was called to spiritually father or mother others within the small group. Carl started out this way, first as a grassroots father who received valuable training in the small group. Thousands of churches all over the world are returning to the biblical pattern of encouraging small group meetings in homes within the congregation. These cell group leaders and assistant leaders see their group members as a spiritual family who are in need of nurturing and training to become spiritual fathers. Grassroots parents give basic training to their small group. Cell ministry without the dynamic of spiritual fathering and mothering will quickly become a dead church program.

Local church fathers

Our church grew rapidly with grassroots parents reproducing themselves over and over again. We needed another kind of spiritual father to accommodate the swell. We began to develop the next level of spiritual fathers—*pastors and elders.* Carl moved on to this aspect of spiritual fatherhood because God entrusted him with the responsibility to oversee not only one or two spiritual families (cells) at a time, but a whole team of spiritual fathers and mothers (cell group leaders) in the church. Now he was a pastor-father of a congregation consisting of many cells.

This new branch of spiritual fathering and mothering released us to become eight congregations in Pennsylvania and three in other nations. We viewed the leadership (eldership) of these eleven congregations as "local church fathers." They regarded their church not as a meeting, but as a family of believers meeting in cell groups. They were called to oversee the many spiritual families (cell groups) and cell leaders within their church.

A local church pastor has the heart of a shepherd to care for the cell leaders, who in turn care for his sheep, the congregation. When I served as a senior pastor, I often told our team of pastors, "You should not be in your office all day: you should be out spiritually parenting small group leaders."

A pastor should meet with the small group leaders on their turf. On occasion, when I served as a pastor, I had three breakfasts in one morning as I met individually with three cell leaders in a restaurant close to where they all lived. One time, I hopped on a cell leader's tractor and spent time with him as he plowed his field! Spending time parenting small group leaders in the church like this raises future spiritual fathers.

Some of these future spiritual fathers will eventually desire their own families. They will become church planters beginning a whole new branch of the family, a new church, that will meet the needs of the new generation coming into the kingdom of God. A pastor who has the heart of a father is more concerned about the welfare of his spiritual sons and daughters than his own personal vision for his congregation.

Carl Jenks is a father-leader like this. When I spoke at Carl's church in North Chili, New York, I witnessed an amazing phenomenon. The church is in the midst of raising funds to build a 1,200-seat auditorium but they recently sent out two new church planters and teams to start new churches. They could send out these teams because two men in the congregation had a call from God to plant new churches within their home communities. Carl Jenks is an example of the new generation of fathers God is developing among us who will not hold back their spiritual children to fulfill their own vision. In the midst of raising money required for a building project, new leaders have been sent out with a blessing to start new churches.

Apostolic fathers

When our church was fifteen years old, we had grown to a point that we knew we had to move to another branch of spiritual fathering to accomplish what God had called us to do. The vision the Lord had given us, "to build a relationship with Jesus, with one another, and reach the world from house to house, city to city, and nation to nation" could not be fulfilled under our current church structure. So we gave our church away!

We had always preached about empowering and releasing individual believers to their full potential, and now we gave that freedom to each of the congregations of our "mega-church" in rural Pennsylvania. We were convinced the Lord was asking us to release each congregation, giving them the option of joining the DOVE Christian Fellowship International family of churches and ministries or connecting to another part of the body of Christ. The eight congregations and most of the overseas church plants expressed a desire to stay together and partner with the DCFI family of churches worldwide.

Our transition as a church required us to form an apostolic council to give spiritual oversight to the leadership of all of the self-governing congregations. This team birthed a new category of spiritual fathering in the church—*apostolic fathers.* The spiritual fathers who serve on our Apostolic Council give spiritual oversight, protection, and serve as an outside court of appeal to the senior leader and to the leadership teams of our local churches.

C. Peter Wagner, in his book *The New Apostolic Churches,* calls this apostolic movement with apostolic fathers, "The New Apostolic Reformation." He says this new work of God is "changing the shape of Protestant Christianity around the world...traditional Christianity starts with the present situation and focuses on the past. New apostolic Christianity starts with the present situation and focuses on the future."[3] These new apostolic leaders are dedicated to releasing the people of their congregations to do the ministry of the church.

Like any healthy, natural father who relates to his married child, apostolic fathers influence rather than control. These seasoned apostolic fathers mentor and coach pastors of local churches, and they do so by developing supportive relationships with local church elders. The relationship is a God-ordained relationship, not built through denominational structure. More than twenty apostolic fathers are mentioned in the New Testament; Paul, Barnabas, Silas, James, Timothy and many others had responsibility before the Lord to serve the leadership of the early church. Paul's letters are an example of New Testament apostolic spiritual fathering.

I am especially sensitive to this kind of spiritual fathering because during the majority of the years while I was pastoring a church, I did not have anyone to father me. I paid dearly for this. The Lord, however, is always redemptive. He has used the lack that I experienced to cause me to be sensitive to Him to train apostolic fathers who will help to parent this next generation of church leadership.

There are many lonely leaders today—pastors and pastors' wives of both independent churches and denominational churches—who are looking for apostolic spiritual fathers and mothers. The Lord is hearing their cries, and raising up many apostolic fathers in our day who have a call and passion to serve these fatherless ministers in local churches. These ministers need a more mature minister to sit with them regularly, to listen to them, to cry with them, and to coach them. Apostolic fathers will encourage them to press into the Lord and to trust His Word. Many pastors have had a hard time fathering future leaders in their churches, because they themselves have never been fathered. The only models of spiritual leadership they have seen are those who lead by hands-on management and control from the top.

The Lord is placing the lonely in families

Churches that have embarked on cell ministry without understanding and living out spiritual fathering have only started another religious cell group program. The church is built through our Lord Jesus Christ by God-ordained relationships.

In Psalms 68:6 the Lord tells us he is placing "the lonely in families" (NIV). The Lord is restoring spiritual parenting to His church today to meet the needs of lonely new believers, lonely church members, lonely small group leaders, and lonely pastors. Recently, I was in Bulgaria and a pastor told me as we drove to the airport, "The loneliness I have had in my heart for years is gone. The Lord has provided spiritual fathers for me."

An apostolic father will have a heart to help bring into completion (not compete with) the ministry the Lord is building in a local church. He will be an equipper and encourager who comes alongside the pastor to see the pastor's vision fulfilled. As a representative of Jesus Christ, he comes with a servant's heart and has a desire to see his son far exceed him in ministry.

While I was in South Africa speaking at a conference, I was approached by a gentleman who asked me if I knew much about apostles and apostolic ministry. He was not clear about apostolic ministry in the church today and simply wanted my opinion. "In the last few years," he said, "along with a team of friends, we started 90 churches. We look after these churches and maintain a relationship with the leaders. Is that apostolic ministry?" I assured him it was! These churches were built by relationship, where the apostolic fathers gave loving oversight to those who were pastoring each of the 90 churches. This young Christian leader saw these churches as a cluster of spiritual families, and he was in a place to help them grow healthy and strong.

Each congregation, denomination, movement, and "stream" within the body of Christ is very important to the Lord. We are all needed and should strive to work together because we are the family of God. However, regardless of what you may want to call them in your denomination or movement, pastors and leaders throughout the body of Christ are crying out for apostolic fathers. Denominations that begin to implement the truth of spiritual fathering within their denominations will find a fresh wind of the Spirit blowing across their denomination. However, this must be built by relationship, not by bureaucratic hierarchy.

One of the reasons for the lack of apostolic fathers in the body of Christ has been a lack of financial support. In the same way that believers in local churches give tithes to support their local leadership, many churches throughout the world are giving tithes to support the team of apostolic fathers who serve them.

Fathers of regions

The Lord is doing an awesome thing in our day. He is restoring the unity He prayed for in John 17:21: "That they all may be one, as You, Father, are in Me, and I in You; that they also may be one in Us, that the world may believe that You sent Me." Walls that have divided denominations and churches for centuries are coming down throughout the world at an intense rate. Pastors in the same town who never knew one another are now finding each other, praying together regularly, and supporting each other. This kind of church unity is exciting!

Over the next years, there will be an emergence of spiritual leaders from various backgrounds and denominations who will form teams of spiritual leadership who serve various cities and regions of the world.

There will be apostolic fathers serving towns, cities, and regions. They will no longer only think in terms of pastoring their own church, but will think and pray in terms of sensing a responsibility with other fellow servant leaders throughout the body of Christ to pastor their region. This will not compete with their denominations, but will bring wholeness. Although these "fathers of the region" will be concerned about unity, it will not be their main focus. Their main focus will be on the Lord and on His mandate to reach the lost as the Lord brings in His harvest.

When LaVerne and I were married in 1971, we found we had two sets of relationships to pursue and maintain: those on her side of the family and those on mine. Both were important. Every denomination and church movement has a redemptive purpose from the Lord that a region needs. We need to maintain healthy relationships with the apostolic fathers of our church movement, and we also need to keep healthy relationships with the spiritual fathers of our region. When Ford Corporation runs a car through the assembly line at Detroit, parts have been gathered from companies from all over the world. These parts are assembled at Detroit. God has brought denominations and church families from all over the world to your town or city, as He assembles His church in your city. Each church and ministry should be honored. As we walk together in unity in our region, the Lord will command a blessing.

Unity among pastors and church leaders in the same region constantly surfaces as one of the most important prerequisites for revival to come to any town or city. Apostolic fathers serving towns, cities, and regions set the stage for unity that brings revival. There are apostolic fathers who serve in leadership over movements, and apostolic leaders who serve in leadership over regions. Some apostolic leaders serve in both areas of leadership. These fathers are not self-appointed, but are recognized by the leadership of the church and ministries in the region they represent.

The fivefold fathers

Calvin Greiner, a prophetic teacher from Manheim, Pennsylvania, after serving for a season as a senior pastor, now ministers in churches of many denominations as a trans-local fivefold minister.

God is raising modern-day fivefold ministers, like Calvin, in His church today: "And He Himself gave some to be apostles, some prophets, some evangelists, and some pastors and teachers, for the equipping of the saints for the work of ministry, for the edifying of the body of Christ" (Ephesians 4:11-12).

The origins of the fivefold ministry gifts are from Jesus Christ. Jesus is the:

- Apostle of apostles, "As the Father has sent Me, I also send you" (John 20:21b). In the Greek, an ambassador of the gospel who is sent out is called *apostolos*.

- Prophet of prophets, "His disciples did not understand these things at first..." (John 12:16). As a prophet, Jesus explained what they didn't understand.

- Evangelist of evangelists, "I am the way the truth and the life, no one comes to the Father except through Me" (John 14:6).

- Teacher of teachers, "You call Me Teacher and Lord, and you say well, for so I am" (John 13:13).

- Pastor of pastors, "I am the good shepherd" (John 10:11a).

Calvin has tapped into the potential of spiritual fathering that is desperately missing in the body of Christ. Every week, he trains potential fivefold ministers how to teach God's Word. He is what I call a "fivefold father." He knows that if he trains a few young teachers and prophets who, in turn, train others, the reproduction potential is staggering.

Fivefold spiritual fathers and mothers train the next generation in their specific gifts and calling. As apostles, prophets, evangelists, pastors and teachers, they speak with the Lord's authority because they represent one of the ministry gifts of Jesus Christ. The Lord validates them by the evidence of spiritual fruit, changed lives and signs following their ministry such as miracles. They are recognized by local church leadership and released into ministry.

Apostolic fathers train younger apostolic ministers, prophetic fathers train younger prophets in prophetic ministry and so on, so that the body of Christ is equipped, encouraged and comes to maturity. The Lord sent these fivefold parents (representing specific gifts) to us that we might be complete, lacking nothing. Their goal as fivefold ministers is to train, equip and prepare the Lord's body to be functional in everyday life as ministers of the gospel of Christ. They mentor future leadership after their own kind and help them avoid many of the pitfalls of past generations. They train their spiritual sons and daughters to minister with the supernatural power of the Holy Spirit.

Importance of spiritual gifts in ministry

Not every believer will operate as a fivefold father in the ministry of apostle, prophet, evangelist, pastor, or teacher. However, each believer can minister with the supernatural power of the Holy Spirit in the gifts of the Spirit according to I Corinthians 12:7-11 (word of wisdom, word of knowledge, faith, gifts of healings, working of miracles, prophecy, discerning of spirits, different kinds of tongues, and the interpretation of tongues). Dennis DeGrasse, in his book *The Gifts of the Holy Spirit*, reminds us of the importance of these spiritual gifts in today's church:

> Sadly, some modern-day saints believe the gifts of the Spirit were for the "good old days" of early church Christianity and not for today's Christian. They claim the early Christians *needed* His supernatural power for the overwhelming task they faced as a fledgling movement, and when they no longer needed the gifts to illuminate and magnify the proclamation of the gospel, the gifts ceased.
>
> In studying church history, however, there are many evidences of the manifestations of the gifts of the Spirit down through the ages. Although at dark times in church history, they may have been rare, the gifts never ceased. If the supernatural gifts of the Spirit were not highly visible in the church throughout the ages, it was not because God removed them from the scene or believers no longer needed them. Their rarity simply represented failure on the part of God's people.
>
> Believers often reclaim the New Testament dynamics of moving in the gifts during times of renewal in church history. This brings new life to the church...I believe today's church is once again hungry for His supernatural power in order to live victoriously. We need the gifts today more than ever before because we need His power!

Paul told the saints at Corinth to pay attention to the gifts of the Spirit: "Now concerning spiritual gifts, brethren, I do not want you to be ignorant" (I Corinthians 12:1). We cannot afford to ignore or be ignorant of these important gifts because we desperately need them in order to function effectively for Christ.

Another time, Paul encourages the church to "earnestly desire spiritual gifts" (I Corinthians 14:1). God made sure that they were recorded in His Word for our benefit. They are not just an interesting historical fact, but are available for us today.

The nine gifts of the Holy Spirit cannot be earned—they are freely given by God to His children. They are not the result of personal righteousness or come from exercising strenuous spiritual discipline. They are given freely at the sovereign will of God. The purpose of the nine gifts is for ministry to others. As members of the body of Christ, we should expect God to manifest His gifts through us to a person in need.[4]

Spiritual gifts are like dynamite, they are powerful for good or can be twisted and misunderstood by the enemy for evil. The fivefold fathers are being raised up by the Lord in our day to prepare mature fivefold ministers operating in the gifts of the Holy Spirit. I believe they will follow the pattern of John Wesley's circuit riders who traveled on horseback from house to house and from congregation to congregation to minister to God's people, training them for His service.

Restoring both the power and fruit of the Spirit

We need all of these various kinds of spiritual parenting in each area of church life in these critical last days as the Lord restores the truth of Malachi 4:6. There must be a balance of both the power and fruit of the Spirit to accomplish it.

Much of the impartation for both the power and the fruit of the Spirit comes through personal spiritual parenting. Rick Joyner recently wrote this prophetic word about the church:

"Often those who know the power of the Spirit do not display much of the fruit of the Spirit, and those who have the fruit of the Spirit do not know the power of the Spirit. That will change in a great way...Those with the fruit of the Spirit will start walking in power, and those with the power will start having the fruit of the Spirit. God is the Almighty, but He is also love, and for the church to be a true reflection of Him, we must manifest both His power and His love. As these two are joined, great advances for the gospel will be ignited."[5]

Spiritual fathering is a part of the Lord's plan to restore both the power of the Spirit and the fruit of the Spirit to His church. Fruit must be cultivated to grow. Let's humble ourselves and learn to look to others who have cultivated the soil of our lives as they parented us, so we can bring forth fruit that will remain for the next generation of leadership.

God has divine plans for our lives. I was a chicken farmer when the Lord called LaVerne and me to serve as spiritual parents to new believers. He was training us in the basics of spiritual fathering and mothering. We had no idea then as to where the Lord was taking us.

Our God is no respecter of persons. Some of us are housewives, others are high-school students, others run corporations or work in law firms, factories, or department stores. The call is the same. He is calling you and me to become spiritual parents. And, as you'll see in the next chapter, we have distinct fields in which to work.

Notes

[1] Dr. Mark Hanby, *You Have Not Many Fathers*, (Shippensburg, Pennsylvania: Destiny Image Publishers, Inc., 1996), p. 174.

[2] Larry Kreider, *House to House*, (Ephrata, Pennsylvania: House to House Publications, 1995).

[3] C. Peter Wagner, *The New Apostolic Churches,* (Ventura, California: Regal Books, 1998), pp. 18, 20.

[4] Dennis DeGrasse, *The Gifts of the Holy Spirit*, (Ephrata, Pennsylvania: House to House Publications, 1999), pp. 10-11.

[5] Rick Joyner, *Prophetic Bulletin*, January 1999, (Charlotte, North Carolina: Morning Star Publications), p.1.

CHAPTER 13

Fathering
Your Fields

Spiritual fathers and mothers have a
distinct sphere of influence

I live in the fertile agricultural area of Lancaster County, Pennsylvania with its lush green and golden fields of corn, alfalfa, barley and wheat covering the landscape. Whenever I fly over the area, I am amazed at the patterns the fields of all shapes and sizes display with their unique colors and boundaries. Each field represents a particular crop waiting to be harvested. This diversity of crops in carefully cultivated fields gives us the distinction of producing more agricultural products and yielding more food than any other non-irrigated county in our nation.

Do you know that you have specific fields of ministry, unique to you, that have been assigned to you by the Lord? These fields, dotting the landscape of your life, are your spheres of influence, responsibility and anointing.

The Greek word translated *field (sphere)* in II Corinthians 10, is *metron* which is *a measure of activity that defines the limits of one's power and influence.* Every Christian has various spiritual fields that give him or her great opportunity to experience God's blessing and empowerment: "We, however, will not boast beyond measure, but within the limits of the sphere which God appointed us—a sphere which especially includes you" (II Corinthians 10:13).

If you are married, you have a field of ministry with your spouse. If you have children, it extends to your family. If you lead a cell group, you have another sphere of influence that includes the spiritual responsibility you have for the cell members. Your involvement in your church gives you a sphere in which to experience God's blessing. Your community is yet another sphere. As a member of your neighborhood, you have a field of ministry on your street as you pray for your neighbors to come to Christ. Your workplace provides an additional sphere of influence. As a spiritual parent, the Lord gives you spheres of influence to bless and strengthen the lives of your spiritual children. Everyone has several different areas in which they have the influence and power to decide what goes on within that field.

A person who wants to have prosperous fields of ministry understands that each of his fields has certain limitations and boundaries. These boundaries give protection to the field and must be carefully and prayerfully respected. When I was a farmer, I did not have the option of taking my tractor over to plow in my neighbor's field and then deciding what crops he would plant. That was up to him. It was his field! I also never contemplated going into his field and planting my seed. This would be counterproductive because I did not own that field and could never claim the harvest from it. I planted, cultivated and harvested crops that fell within my own property lines.

Where I live, farmers often post several "No Trespassing" signs at the edges of their fields, meant to deter hunters from tramping across their fields during hunting season. In life, there are often disastrous results when someone trespasses on another's field.

You have only to look at the divorce statistics in today's world to see the trail of devastation left when a married person steps across his or her marriage boundaries into someone else's marriage. A police officer works within the boundaries of his jurisdiction. He can arrest only those criminals within the area of his legal authority. As a parent, you have authority and responsibility for your own family's field. You cannot tell your neighbors how to raise their children because you do not have authority in their home. The stereotypical mother-in-law gets a bad rap as an interfering, meddlesome creature who disrupts her children's marriage. This kind of intruding mother-in-law moves beyond her area of authority and infringes into the marriage relationship that belongs to her children.

Your field has boundaries

Like the farming fields of my county, clearly distinguishable by color, size and boundaries, ministry fields also have certain boundaries and size. As spiritual parents, we must have a clear understanding of the boundaries of our fields. We should never presume to speak into another's life unless he has opened his boundaries to us. In other words, we cannot intrude into the life of another until there is a relationship of trust built which opens the door for us to speak into his field.

Of course, if a spiritual son clearly has sin in his life, we need to lovingly appeal to him according to Matthew 18:15-17. Even then, we must be careful to allow our spiritual sons and daughters to take responsibility for their own boundaries and personal choices they make. They must learn to live with the consequences of their own choices; spiritual parents are in place to encourage, not dictate or control.

In Genesis 1:26, God gave Adam and Eve authority over the whole world, but they had to prove their stewardship in the Garden of Eden first. We know what happened when Satan came into Adam and Eve's field and they listened to his lies—they surrendered their authority to Satan, and pain and death fell on them and the world God had made beautiful.

Do not surrender your field to another. If someone feels they have a "word from God" for you, remember, it must be tested (I Thessalonians 5:20-21). Test it with the Word of God, with the godly advice of spiritual fathers the Lord has placed in your life, and with the peace of Christ that rules in your heart (Colossians 3:15).

Several years ago when I was serving as a pastor in Pennsylvania, a Christian speaker gave a specific "prophetic" word to me and to our leadership team while he was ministering at various congregations in our area. He described to us something he was convinced the Lord was leading our church to do. We prayed and considered his "word," and realized that in order for us to fulfill it, we could not keep our commitment to rent one of our buildings to a Christian group in our area. It would be an issue of integrity for us. We thanked this man for sharing with us what he believed the Lord was saying and told him that it may be a timing issue. Perhaps we could still do what he suggested at another time.

The next day, I received a phone call from him, and he gave me another "prophetic" word (a curse, really) for our church. He even used the scriptures to pronounce this curse. That evening we called all of our local leaders together in united prayer. Since this man was simply visiting our field and did not have authority in our field, we knew he was not responsible for our field. It was a field that the Lord had given to us. We took authority over this curse and received the Lord's protection in Jesus' name. We avoided a potentially devastating "prophetic word" for our church by understanding our own particular field and its boundaries. A few days later, I spoke with a missionary friend who was serving in the same nation this "prophet" had come from. We learned that this man had divided many churches in his homeland by prophecies that overstepped the boundaries of his authority with his attempt at manipulation.

Praying within your spiritual field

Another type of unhealthy control can even occur in prayer. For example, if an intercessor in a church begins to pray for his pastor to "understand [a certain truth] like I understand it," he is attempting to change the pastor rather than allowing God Himself to impress a particular truth on the pastor's heart.

Praying for things to go the way we think they should go rather than the way the person responsible for that field is led by the Spirit to take them can be dangerous. If intercessors are not taught about fields of ministry, this kind of control becomes a type of "spiritual witchcraft." I have ministered to many church leaders who were under tremendous spiritual oppression, because people in the church were praying according to their own agendas rather than praying for God's agenda. True spiritual fathers, with their maturity and experience, need to help leaders and other believers discern the source of this oppression.

You will not go wrong when you pray the scriptures. Pray like Paul, "For this reason I bow my knees to the Father of our Lord Jesus Christ, from whom the whole family in heaven and on earth is named, that He would grant you, according to the riches of His glory, to be strengthened with the might of His Spirit in the inner man, that Christ may dwell in your hearts through faith; that you, being rooted and grounded in love, may comprehend with all the saints what is the width and length and depth and height—to know the love of Christ which passes knowledge; that you may be filled with all the fullness of God. Now to Him who is able to do exceedingly abundantly above all that we ask or think, according to the power that works in us, to Him be glory in the church by Christ Jesus throughout all ages, world without end. Amen" (Ephesians 3:14-21).

Honoring the fields of others

Paul, the apostle, understood his sphere of influence and reminded the Corinthians that he only operates in the sphere in which God appointed him. He did not go around troubling churches founded by others. He only boasted of the Corinthian church because he was responsible before the Lord for them:

"We, however, will not boast beyond measure, but within the limits of the sphere which God appointed us—a sphere which especially includes you. For we are not extending ourselves beyond our sphere (thus not reaching you), for it was to you that we came with the gospel of Christ; not boasting of things beyond measure, that is, in other men's labors, but having hope, that as your faith is increased, we shall be greatly enlarged by you in our sphere" (II Corinthians 10:13-15).

Paul was careful not to take the credit or responsibility for another person's field of ministry. He knew his own sphere's "shape and color" and operated within God's authority and anointing for its oversight.

I preach at a different church in a different part of the world nearly every week. I always remember: I am serving in someone else's field. I am helping a pastor and a team of church leadership to build in their particular field.

Sadly, over the years, many who claimed to be anointed and spiritual did not properly understand serving within the field of another. Sometimes pastors of churches have had to take months to "clean up" from various things that were said or "prophesied" by a visiting speaker that were not edifying to the church. This will not happen if we walk within our own fields of ministry and honor the fields of others.

Grace for your field

Along with the authority a spiritual father has within the boundaries of his field, a portion of grace is given to do the job. *Grace* is often described as *the free unmerited favor of God on the undeserving and ill-deserving*, but it also can be defined as *the desire and the power to do God's will*. It is like a divine energy that the Holy Spirit releases in our lives. It helps us to victoriously accomplish a task within our fields of ministry.

How do we know that God gives a person grace to operate within his field of ministry? The word *metron* has a slightly different meaning in Ephesians 4:7: "But to each one of us grace has been given as Christ apportioned it." Here the word *apportioned* is a translation of the same word *metron* found in II Corinthians 10:13. So, it would follow that for each metron or field of ministry, there is a special grace given for it.

Since we all have different-sized fields, God apportions grace in varying amounts according to what we need. Spiritual fathers and mothers will know how many spiritual children they can mentor at a time, and they will receive grace to do it. If spiritual parents get out of the field of ministry in which they are assigned, they get out of God's grace, and that is not a good place to be!

Spiritual parents will caution their spiritual children to remain in their fields of ministry and thus remain in the grace of God. Did you ever wonder why some pastors have large churches and others have smaller churches? Is it prayer? Although prayer is extremely important, I do not think this is neccesarily always the reason. I know of pastors of small churches who have a much more effective prayer life than some with large churches. God simply gives some pastors grace for larger churches, and others grace for smaller churches. The size of our church is not the issue; the issue is obedience and training and releasing spiritual children (John 14:15).

I was speaking at a leadership conference a few years ago, and joined the group of about 500 pastors and Christian leaders in the audience for an evening service. The moderator of the conference asked a friend of mine to stand. I had talked to this man earlier in the conference. He pastored a church of 50 people in Dallas, Texas. He had served as a pastor in churches in various states over the years. The moderator then asked every man to stand in the auditorium who had been a spiritual son or had been influenced by this pastor. Men stood up all over the auditorium! I was deeply moved. Then I sensed the Lord's still small voice, "That's success." Success does not necessarily have anything to do with the size of a church or ministry. Success is loving God enough to obey Him as a spiritual parent.

Don't plow in your son's field

In the mid 1970's a movement called the "discipleship movement" was popular. Good discipleship principles were sometimes overshadowed by unhealthy one-on-one relationships where leaders required those under their authority to get their approval before making decisions such as dating, marriage, and even visiting relatives during holidays! In some cases, families were split apart and lives turned upside down.

This movement led to unbiblical obedience to human leaders, and in some cases, the leaders twisted the biblical principle of accountability by stepping into others' fields and attempting to make their decisions for them. Occasionally, believers moved halfway across the country to follow their spiritual parents to a new location when they moved.

To say we will *always* have a close relationship with someone can become bondage. We must take the attitude of "if the Lord wills!" James 4:13-15 (NIV) tells us: "Now listen, you who say, 'Today or tomorrow we will go to this or that city, spend a year there, carry on business and make money.' Why, you do not even know what will happen tomorrow. What is your life? You are a mist that appears for a little while and then vanishes. Instead, you ought to say, 'If it is the Lord's will, we will live and do this or that.'"

We do not know if we will maintain a long-term, close fathering or mothering relationship with the spiritual children we are now mentoring. This is up to the Lord, not up to us.

Those who found themselves in these situations in the 1970's were involved in what could be called "unholy covenants." True spiritual fathers never ask their sons to make unholy covenants or make decisions for them. Spiritual fathers and mothers will never seek to control their spiritual children in this manner.

A holy covenant vs. an unholy covenant

A holy covenant is a promise or undertaking on the part of God. The only covenants that are holy and last for a lifetime are (1) the covenant I have with Christ to serve Him completely, (2) the covenant I have with my wife to love her and cherish her "until death do us part," and (3) the covenant I have with the body of Christ to love her and be a blessing to the Lord's bride. We must be careful to never get involved in unholy covenants.

So what is an unholy covenant? While a holy covenant is a promise on the part of God, an unholy covenant is made with a person or group that hinders one from obeying the Holy Spirit's leading in his life. For example, some believers were asked to stay at a certain church their entire lifetimes because they were "in covenant" with the leadership. This is unholy and unhealthy. We cannot be sure of the time frame of serving with those in our current church.

In a spiritual fathering relationship, if the Lord calls either the father or the son to serve elsewhere in another field, we need to release them and help them find their place of most fruitful ministry.

Your field yields fruit

When you are cultivating your field within its boundaries and receiving God's grace for the field, it will yield fruit: "Lord, you have assigned me my portion and my cup; you have made my lot secure. The boundary lines have fallen for me in pleasant places; surely I have a delightful inheritance" (Psalm 16:5-6 NIV).

Rather than limit us, boundary lines allow us to be fruitful in our spheres of influence. The fields to which God assigns us are protected, secure places of learning. We grow and learn how to receive our inheritance within that field. Within the boundaries of our fields, we will receive rich blessings because we are where the Lord wants us to be. We will know when we are in the right spiritual parenting relationship(s) because they will yield fruit!

God determines and expands our fields

Be responsible within your present field. Build it, and God will enhance it. Allow God to promote you. If you are called to be a spiritual father or mother to someone, or to start a cell group or plant a new church, remember, timing is everything. Ecclesiastes 8:5-6 indicates that there is a proper time and procedure for every matter. David is the classic example—he was called and anointed to be king, but there was already a king. David did not seize or attempt to overthrow authority. He allowed God to promote him in His time.

Spiritual fathers should help their sons determine their fields and encourage them to allow the Lord to promote them into other fields when change is on the horizon. The sons may not have the maturity to see this. It is one way fathers can protect their sons.

Delegate authority in your field

Another way to father spiritual sons is to help them delegate authority to the sons they are raising. You can temporarily delegate to others the authority God has given you in a field of ministry. For example, when parents are away from home, they might ask the oldest child to be responsible for the house. This child has received delegated authority for his parent's field.

I Timothy 1:1-4 describes how Timothy was assigned a portion of Paul's authority in Ephesus, even to the point of bringing correction to false teachers and doctrines. Pastors of churches assign authority to cell leaders to lead a cell group, and cell leaders work within the field they are assigned. They do not take authority in other areas of the church. This would cause confusion.

It is only the Lord who empowers us and gives us the anointing to rule our fields. In Matthew 10:1, Jesus gave authority to His disciples as He was opening up a new field for them. He did not send them out without first giving them the delegated authority. With this delegated authority, they would operate in His power and love to change the world.

Allow God to assign you fields through His delegated authority with the expectation that He will expand them as you are faithful. You have *stewardship* of the field, *not ownership*. A teller at a bank does not own the money she handles day after day, but she is a steward of it. Our God owns all spiritual fields. We are only stewards.

A symptom that you are taking ownership rather than stewardship occurs if you get discouraged when someone leaves your field. For instance, if you are leading a small group and someone leaves the group, or if your spiritual son or daughter moves on to another mentoring relationship, you must realize that God brings people to your field, and God can lead them away. This is His field, and these are His people, not ours. We must get a broader picture of the greater body of Christ and rejoice, rather than be threatened, when "our family" (those we have mentored and trained) is released to other fields (churches and ministries).

Do not tolerate the enemy's activity in your field

Paul had a sense of responsibility for the Corinthian church (II Corinthians 11:28-29). We, too, must be responsible and, as spiritual fathers and mothers, stand in the gap and intercede for our spiritual children. Ezekiel 22:30 gives us a picture of prayer warfare as a believer standing in the gap between God's mercy and man's need. God has given you the authority to intercede in this way.

As we parent our spiritual children, we need to stand in the gap for them and refuse to allow the enemy to rob them when sin creates a gap in their lives. As spiritual parents, we must take possession of our inheritance by interceding diligently. Our intercession restricts and destroys satanic strongholds and evil forces of the enemy and allows the Holy Spirit to bring godly influences into our spiritual children's lives.

A complete discussion of fields of ministry and their importance to church leaders is found in Appendix A (page 169).

Take possession of your fields

By way of summary, we must recognize what fields are and faithfully work within them. It is important to teach spiritual moms and dads, cell leaders, church leadership, and future leadership how fields of ministry work. You may be a grassroots spiritual parent, a pastor serving as a spiritual parent, or an apostolic spiritual parent. No matter what type of spiritual parent you are—the responsibility is yours for your fields of ministry, large or small. You are given responsibility and oversight for multiple fields of ministry: your home, church, business and community. These are your fields of assignment from the Lord. Know what your fields are. Your fields have certain boundaries, giving them size and shape. As a spiritual father or mother, rise up in faith and possess the fields the Lord has given to you!

Take possession of your fields, working faithfully in His grace and respecting others' fields around you. Christ has entrusted your fields to you. Walk in His grace and produce a diversity of crops in carefully cultivated fields. This will give you the distinction of yielding more fruit than you could ever have imagined!

As you work in your fruit-bearing fields, it is paramount that you know how to make wise decisions. In the next chapter, you will learn how to impart biblical decision-making principles to your spiritual children.

CHAPTER 14

Fathers Teach Their Sons to Make Decisions

Decision-making principles for spiritual parents to impart

E very family makes decisions that affect their family in different ways. In some families, Dad simply makes the decisions for the family. Other families find Dad and Mom working together in decision-making. And in other cases, the children seem to run the house. How do we make decisions according to a biblical pattern as spiritual parents?

Why is it so important for church fathers to learn how to make wise judgments in decision-making? It is important because leaders of all kinds must lead as fathers, humbly working together with others to make solid, biblical decisions. In this way, fathers will honor and bless those whom they serve.

Let's look at the first century church and see what they did when they faced a crisis in Acts 15. From this chapter, we learn how spiritual fathers and mothers can make decisions that honor the Lord's voice and value each member of the family. The scriptural principles in this section apply to all levels of spiritual fathering and mothering and spiritual families.

A model for decision-making

In Acts 15, we are given a model for healthy decision-making. In this particular church crisis, a group of Pharisee believers from Jerusalem visited the church in Antioch and objected to the Gentiles coming into the church without submitting to the Jewish rite of circumcision.

Paul and Barnabas were sent to serve on a council at the Jerusalem church along with the other apostles and elders to resolve this matter because of the heated debate that ensued in the church:

> So, being sent on their way by the church, they [Paul and Barnabas] passed through Phoenicia and Samaria, describing the conversion of the Gentiles; and they caused great joy to all the brethren. And when they had come to Jerusalem, they were received by the church and the apostles and the elders; and they reported all things that God had done with them. But some of the sect of the Pharisees who believed rose up, saying, "It is necessary to circumcise them, and to command them to keep the law of Moses" (verses 3-5).

As the apostles and elders came together in Jerusalem to consider the matter, there was much dispute. Peter rose up and said to them:

> "Men and brethren, you know that a good while ago God chose among us, that by my mouth the Gentiles should hear the word of the gospel and believe. So God, who knows the heart, acknowledged them by giving them the Holy Spirit, just as He did to us, and made no distinction between us and them, purifying their hearts by faith" (verses 7-9).

Peter reminded these Jewish believers that they were saved by faith and faith alone just as the Gentiles were. Paul and Barnabas testified next:

> Then all the multitude kept silent and listened to Barnabas and Paul declaring how many miracles and wonders God had worked through them among the Gentiles (verse 12).

After Peter, Paul and Barnabas had their say, James, the head elder and apostolic leader of the Jerusalem church spoke up. The early church leaders trusted James to hear what the Lord was saying to them because they were in his "field" of authority and responsibility.

First of all, James reviewed what he had heard from various leaders throughout the meeting together. Then he quoted from the scriptures. Finally, He spoke up in favor of accepting the uncircumcised Gentiles:

Therefore I judge that we should not trouble those from among the Gentiles who are turning to God (verse 19).

The apostles, elders and the whole congregation agreed and decided to send delegates to Antioch and throughout the churches that had been planted to report this decision with an "acceptance letter." A church doctrinal issue was resolved! What can we learn from this story, and how was such a volatile issue of early church doctrine resolved?

Principles to make father-like decisions

I believe this early church issue was resolved because God's leaders followed proper, biblical decision-making principles. As we look at this story carefully, we see three principles of godly leadership and decision-making. I believe the combined strengths of these three decision-making principles will help us make wise father-like decisions at any level of leadership.

The three principles are very simple: (1) God speaks through a leader (father), (2) God speaks through a team, and (3) God speaks through His people.

Trouble often comes when one of these principles is given greater precedence than the others. Practicing only one of these principles is like driving in a rut on the side of the road rather than utilizing the total road. It causes a spiritual parent to lead in a lopsided manner, often making poor decisions. These three principles are meant to complement each other as each level of leadership works together in relationship with one another.

To help us better understand the dynamics between all three principles, let's think for a minute about the options a natural family has if they utilize one or more of these principles while planning a vacation.

Let's say the Mancini family wants to make a decision about where to spend their summer vacation. Who should make the decision? Should the father make a decision to go on a fishing vacation without taking into consideration the rest of his family? Should the family discuss the issue thoroughly and then hopelessly give up the idea entirely when no one can agree? Should the children vote and decide by majority where to go? Or is there a better way?

Read the following decision-making principles, and you decide.

1. A father who leads the way

First of all, let's look at the biblical principle of "God speaking through a father-leader." God always calls and anoints someone to lead the way and speaks through this spiritual father. James was the head elder and apostle at Jerusalem who held this role.

Although God may speak His vision and direction through many, someone is appointed by the Lord to be the primary spokesperson for the vision. He has a responsibility that is a bit greater in seeing the vision fulfilled than the others on the team. You could say James was the *father* or *primary vision carrier* for the group he was leading. He was the one who heard what the Lord was saying through the entire team and made the declaration of what He believed the Lord was saying to the church.

Both the Old and New Testament give numerous examples of this "leader who leads the way" leadership principle—Adam, Noah, Abraham, Joseph, Debra, Gideon, David, Jesus, Peter, James, Paul—the list goes on and on. Moses asked the Lord to appoint a man over the congregation in Numbers 27:16. In the New Testament, in Acts 13:1-4, Barnabas and Saul were sent out with a team to evangelize and plant new churches. By verse thirteen, the Bible says Paul and his companions went to the next city. Paul had already become the clear leader—the primary leader of the team.

In the corporate world, we often call the head leader of a corporation a Chief Executive Officer (CEO). CEO's are responsible for the vision and general oversight of their company—what goes on within its doors, how it will grow and its overall image. They have authority to make the decisions that affect the future of the company. Their leadership is usually equated with power, position or prestige.

Primary church fathers should lead in a totally different manner. Although they are also in positions of authority and are responsible for the people the Lord has placed within their care, they must not lead as domineering CEO's. Leaders who lead as fathers will support their spiritual children in order to see their *children* fulfill *their* dreams and visions. They encourage their children to hear from God and make their own decisions rather than always handing down decisions made at the top.

When primary leaders choose to lead humbly as servants, people following them will be encouraged and trained, by example, to do their jobs with the same spirit—that of a servant. In this way, they can participate fully in the life of the church, becoming spiritual fathers and mothers themselves.

Misguided CEO's often *use* people, but spiritual fathers and mothers *serve* people. A true Christian leader's rights actually decrease as he takes his position of authority, and his responsibilities increase. His rights decrease because Christian leadership involves not power or prestige but servanthood. Servanthood is the mark of a leader deeply committed to the development of others. Servant leadership takes its example from Christ, the master leader, when He demonstrated that He "...did not come to be served, but to serve..." (Mark 10:45).

In a family, fathers should be willing to serve by making final decisions: "For the husband is the head of the wife, as also Christ is head of the church; and He is the Savior of the body" (Ephesians 5:23). In every team, there is always someone the Lord places as leadership in that team. In the case of the husband and wife, the Bible says the husband is the head of the wife. He's the one who is called to love his wife the same way Jesus Christ loves His church and gave His life for it. He is also the one who, in times of crisis, is responsible to make the final decisions in the home.

A few years ago, LaVerne and I came to an impasse in making a decision regarding whether or not one of our children should be enrolled in a public school or a Christian school. We prayed and waited before the Lord for an answer, but could not clearly hear the voice of the Lord. Finally, LaVerne told me, "Honey, you are the head of our home, and I believe you will hear what the Lord is saying in this situation. I will honor your decision." It turned out that the decision I felt God was leading me to make was the right one.

A godly father never throws his weight around as a leader. Paul, the apostle, a respected leader of the early church, set the example of a church leader, not as a boss, but as a servant called by the Lord to be a spiritual father: "Nor did we seek glory from men, either from you or from others, when we might have made demands as apostles of Christ. But we were gentle among you, just as a nursing mother cherishes her own children" (I Thessalonians 2:6-7). Paul's letters to the church were written from a loving spiritual parent's perspective, as he modeled the life of a servant to those he spiritually fathered.

Having said all this, there is a downside when someone leads solely through this principle of decision-making because they can become autocratic. In fact, it can become dangerous. Abuses of this kind of leadership may breed the Jim Jones-type cult leaders, husbands who abuse their wives, or those who believe they have a right to tell others what to do in a way that violates their personal authority and responsibility before the Lord.

Sometimes spiritually immature leaders will shrink back and abdicate their decision-making roles in an attempt to please others and gain approval. Spiritual fathers will encourage their sons to take full responsibility and make decisions based on what God is speaking to them in their hearts. Such decisions should be made after input is given from the team that surrounds them.

2. God calls a team to work together

Although James was the clear leader in Acts 15, it is important to see that as a primary leader, James did not make decisions alone. The other apostles and elders met with him, and they worked together as a team to make a decision. In this way, they were all able to confirm James' final decision as he listened to what the Lord was saying through the entire team. The other apostles and elders were honored because they were involved in the process, and their input was valued.

In families, the Lord has called husbands and wives to submit to each other. God wants husbands and wives to be in unity and work as a team: "Submitting to one another in the fear of God" (Ephesians 5:21).

We see this team leadership modeled many times in both the Old and New Testament. Leaders rarely worked alone, but with a team of leaders who served with them. Moses and Aaron and Miriam worked together as a team in Exodus. Acts 16:4 speaks of *apostles and elders*. In I Peter 5:1, the plural term *elders* is used again. In Titus 1:5, Paul exhorts Titus to appoint elders in every town. Paul and Barnabas appointed elders in every church (Acts 14:23) and worked with them as an eldership team.

Why is it so important to work together as a team? A primary leader has only so many gifts to lead God's people. According to the Bible, no matter how spiritual we think we are, "We know in part and we prophesy in part" (I Corinthians 13:9). A team of leaders will fill in the gaps for the primary leader's limitations and the limitations of other members. Leaders have only a portion of the Lord's wisdom. A leader and his team will listen to what the Lord says through everyone on the team. Then the primary leader will receive the grace to discern what the Lord is saying through the entire team.

When a plane is in flight, the pilot, copilot, and flight attendants all work together as a team. Everything proceeds like clockwork. But this is not true for the whole flight. During take off, landing and times of turbulence, it is the pilot who has to take clear leadership, and everyone on the plane is glad that he does!

Wise team leaders recognize the Lord speaks through each of the team members, and discerns what the Lord is saying through the team (Acts 15). Then he makes the decision and the others on the team affirm his decision.

3. God speaks through His people

Wise parents will listen to their children before making decisions that will affect the family. Spiritual fathers of all kinds will take the time to hear the heart's cry of their spiritual children because they love them, believe the Lord speaks through them, and they want to see them fulfill their destiny in God.

In Acts 6:1-7, leaders we sometimes call *deacons* were chosen. Who chose the deacons? Scripture says *the people* chose seven men, and the apostles appointed them. Wise leaders will listen to what God says through His people. Leaders must value the people they serve!

It is a godly principle to receive input from those you serve before making a decision that affects them. Before an important decision is made, wise church leaders will publicly share the facts and receive godly input so as to leave no room for doubt and discontent among the congregation.

Acknowledge the Lord first

The key to all decision-making is simply knowing that only the Lord can give us wisdom for making decisions. We cannot lean on our own understanding as the writer of Proverbs admonishes us in Proverbs 3:5-6: "Trust in the Lord with all your heart, and lean not on your own understanding; in all your ways acknowledge Him, and He shall direct your paths." We must live in the constant reality that Christ is in our midst, waiting for us to ask Him for wisdom and for direction. Jesus tells us clearly in Matthew 18:19-20 (NIV): "Again, I tell you that if two of you on earth agree about anything you ask for, it will be done for you by my Father in heaven. For where two or three come together in my name, there am I with them."

Combine the strengths—head, shoulders and body

As a leader is constantly acknowledging the Lord, he must make an effort to focus on all three decision-making principles in order to make balanced decisions. There are strengths in all three, and if a leader combines these strengths, he will experience tremendous unity in his sphere of influence.

Sometimes the analogy of "head and shoulders and body" is used to show the combined strengths of all three principles. It helps to explain further how a spiritual father/leader works together with others to hear what the Lord is saying.

In Psalms 133, David is singing a song about unity. At this point in biblical history, the tribes of Israel were united under one head. The blessing of this unity is described as the fragrant holy anointing oil poured upon the head of Aaron, the high priest. It was so plentiful that it ran down his face onto his shoulders and down the garment on his body. God pours out His wisdom on the head which flows to the shoulders and on to the body.

Using the analogy of a head, shoulders and body, regarding balanced decision-making, the head (primary leader) of every team needs to be properly attached to the shoulders (the others on the team) and the body (the people) through a God-ordained relationship of trust and affirmation. If the head is appropriately attached to the shoulders (through relationship, trust, servanthood, prayer and proper communication), and the shoulders properly support and affirm the head, there will be unity, and God will command a blessing as indicated in Psalm 133.

God gives His grace and anointing to the primary leader of the team to hear what He is saying through the entire team. However, if the head is stretched too far from the shoulders (the primary leader is not honoring the team) and makes decisions in an autocratic style, the shoulders (the team) and the body (the people) will experience a pain in the neck. By the same token, if the head is forced down into the shoulders (by the team not honoring the head), the body will again experience a pain in the neck.

I believe that many times, the Lord will give vision to a leader, but the timing is in the hands of the team and the people. It takes time to pray and share so that all three gain a sense of godly stewardship for a decision made.

Unless there is trust established between team members and team leaders, decisions cannot be made effectively. When brothers "dwell together in unity" (Psalms 133:1-3), the Lord commands a blessing. Trust takes time to build in relationships.

The need for additional accountability

While we do our best to implement all three decision-making principles in our relationships on all levels, it is wise to have additional spiritual fathers or mothers for added accountability, especially if problems surface. Spiritual parents of any kind—those in one-on-one spiritual parenting relationships or those in church leadership—should be accountable even for a final decision. This avoids the absolute authority trap. A cell leader, for example receives additional accountability from his church elders. In a one-on-one parenting relationship, another trusted spiritual father or mother can provide accountability for times when help is needed to resolve an issue.

A complete discussion of how these principles apply to church leadership and decision-making is found in Appendix B (page 173).

To summarize

No one is exempt from making decisions. Every person, whether it is in the home, church, workplace, school or community, must make decisions that affect other people. Husbands and wives are appointed by the Lord to give leadership to their families. Pastors and elders are appointed by God to give leadership to their local church. Spiritual parents are appointed to give stewardship to their spiritual sons or daughters. A student who is captain of the football team is a leader to his school's team. In some capacity, most of us are in leadership positions and must know how to make wise biblical decisions.

When we learn how to take responsibility for biblical decision-making, we notice it works in the home, in the church, in a youth group, in a Christian business, and any other place decisions need to be made. God's desire is to "command a blessing" on spiritual fathers and mothers and on spiritual families as we follow His principles of leadership and decision-making.

God wants spiritual fathers and mothers to train their sons and daughters in biblical decision-making so they do not have to fear making decisions that affect others. When sons and daughters learn to hear from their heavenly Father and honor their spiritual fathers and mothers, along with others impacted by their decisions, they will make wise and godly judgments in decision-making.

CHAPTER 15

The Best Is Yet to Come

God is raising up exceptional
spiritual fathers and mothers

A man of God once said, "To do anything less than what you were created to do will bore you." Many are bored in the body of Christ because they are not fulfilling what God created them to become: spiritual parents! Spiritual fathers and mothers rarely get bored. They, instead, have a sense of fulfillment and dignity.

Ibrahim, a journalist from Nairobi, Kenya, knew his people were not living up to their potential. Having a keen interest in spiritual fathering and the cell church concept, he sought for a working model and asked to observe me as I served our new church that was built on the principles of spiritual fathering and small group ministry.

At that time, our church had been birthed as a cell church a few years earlier with three new cells. But we had our setbacks. Instead of multiplying, one cell died. We desperately pleaded for God's help as we reminded our people, "You are ministers, and God desires to use you!" Eventually, faith rose in their hearts, and the Lord used them. People were saved. New believers came to the cells. New leaders were trained. At last—multiplication.

Two cells became four. Four became eight. Eight became sixteen, and sixteen became thirty-two. The church grew rapidly. As pastor, I spent most of my time meeting with cell leaders and discussing the needs and potential in individual cell members. Each leader and I regularly prayed simple faith-filled prayers for each believer in each cell.

These believers were cared for as parents care for their children.

Ibrahim sat watching and listening. Then my African brother opened his heart. Weeping, he unburdened, "Western evangelists come to my nation and hold massive crusades. The TV cameras are rolling. When the evangelist asks my brothers to raise their hands to receive Christ, many respond. The next week, another evangelist comes to town, and many of those same brothers come to the crusade and raise their hands again. My people need a sense of dignity, where every individual believer understands he is important to God and to His purposes. Will you come and help us? We need a new model of church life."

Today, Ibrahim has a vision to train leaders to start cells and new churches throughout Africa. He and his wife, Diane, opened their home for cell ministry. Neighbors and friends received the Lord, and many found a spiritual family. Cells were birthed in neighboring areas of the city, multiplying throughout Kenya and into Uganda.

In 1999, I was in Kenya for their ten-year anniversary of church planting. In their first five years, they grew from one church to two. Then in another five years, they mushroomed to more than 30 churches. God used them as spiritual parents to model a new kind of church life. God's people in these nations have received a new sense of dignity!

Look for a restoration of the fathers

Remember the words of the prophet Malachi: "Behold, I will send you Elijah the prophet before the coming of the great and dreadful day of the Lord. And he will turn the hearts of the fathers to the children, and the hearts of the children to their fathers..." (Malachi 4:5-6). Spiritual fathering is a key to breathing fresh life and vitality into the church.

A few years ago, I was asked to share the vision of the New Testament church in Auckland, New Zealand. There, I met Robert. He listened intently as I spoke about Jesus spending most of His time with the twelve disciples—His spiritual sons. I discussed God's call on every saint to be a minister as stated in Ephesians 4:11-12. I also looked at Acts 2 reflecting the New Testament model of the church as well as speaking on effective small group ministry and spiritual families in today's church.

After thirty minutes, Robert spoke, filled with emotion. "When I was 13 years old, the Lord called me to be a minister. For more than 20 years, I tried to find doors that would open for me to fulfill this call. As

I understood it, the only way to be a minister was to be ordained after completing years of theological training. Sometime back, I led a man to the Lord. I discipled him and watched him grow. It was so fulfilling. I realize tonight, I no longer need to try to be a minister, I am one!" A heavy load dropped from Robert's back. The truth had set him free. Robert realized he could fulfill the Lord's call to minister by discipling a new believer. He had become a spiritual father.

John Wesley, the founder of the Methodist Church, believed that one out of every five persons was a potential leader. Through his exhortation, the Wesleyan movement spread throughout the nations. God's people worked out their calling as ministers and opened their homes for class meetings, similar to cell groups. Each person had a sense of fulfillment and dignity.

The harvest is upon us! Shirley Hampton, who serves in pastoral leadership of Bethel Church of Lititz in Pennsylvania, is a woman of God who uses her prophetic gifting to encourage the church. She fervently believes that "spiritual fathering and mothering will catapult the church into the harvest. God is preparing this support system—spiritual parents with the heart of our heavenly Father—that will birth, nurture, protect, equip and release those coming in." She says, "Church, get ready for changing messy diapers and middle-of-the-night feedings! But, oh the joy that comes as we see those spiritual babes becoming an expression of the Bride who brings our heavenly Bridegroom great pleasure!"

May every saint capture the revelation of the call to minister! Spiritual parents and children together will serve and encourage each other toward maturity. Participating in spiritual parenting is an opportunity to get over boredom and regain a sense of dignity!

Are you a brother or a father?

Ron Myer, a faithful friend and colleague, who has served with me in leadership for more than seventeen years, believes there is a big difference between being a father and being an older brother—especially the kind of brother exemplified in the prodigal son story:

> In many cases, a brother will inspire you, but a father will direct you. A brother may wound you, but a father will heal you. A brother often sees you for who you are, a father sees

your potential. A brother has a tendency to judge you, while a father will lovingly correct you. A brother may condemn you for wasting your inheritance on riotous living, but a father will love you, woo you back home, and restore you.

Aren't you glad the prodigal son ran into his father before his older brother? Had he run into his older brother first, the outcome of the story could have ended much differently.

Here is the good news! The Lord is taking older brothers in our generation and raising them up to become spiritual fathers.

The benefits of obedience

It is not always easy to be a spiritual father. It requires sacrifice, and especially another item in short supply—time. Nevertheless, when we look to the larger purposes God has for our lives, we will see many benefits of our obedience.

Jesus understood that His disciples left their families to follow Him. He reminded them of the benefits of their obedience in Mark 10:29-30: "Assuredly, I say to you, there is not one who has left house or brothers or sisters or father or mother or wife or children or lands, for My sake and the gospel's, who shall not receive a hundredfold now in this time—houses and brothers and sisters and mothers and children and lands, with persecutions—and in the age to come, eternal life."

The person who gives up their comfort zone will gain spiritual children! Jesus assured His disciples they would produce spiritual children, giving them a spiritual heritage to pass on to their spiritual children. This was their reward.

God wants to raise up exceptional spiritual fathers and mothers in our midst, but it requires obedience and sacrifice on our part. Numbers 26:63-65 tells us that out of the thousands of the first generation of Israelites in the wilderness, only Joshua and Caleb were left of that generation to enter the Promised Land because they were the only ones who were obedient and followed the Lord wholeheartedly. Why didn't the rest of their generation make it to the Promised Land? Because they believed a bad report. When the spies came back to Moses and showed them the fruit of the Promised Land, they gave a discouraging report of the giants in the land. They did not believe they could conquer them.

Don't believe a bad report. The enemy will try to get you to believe his lies, "How could I ever be a spiritual parent? I am too busy; I'm not spiritual enough; I made too many mistakes." But the truth is that God has called you. There is a spiritual fathering anointing He will give you to accomplish it. He is releasing this anointing in the church today. It is available to you. We serve a supernatural God who can go way beyond what we can do in the natural.

Sharpen your anointing

In II Kings, 6:1-7 a young man lost his ax head in the waters while cutting down a tree beside a river. Most likely, he walked out into the murky water and searched in vain for the ax head. Finally, knowing he could not accomplish his job without the ax, the young man went to Elisha—the one person he thought could help him in his dilemma.

There may come a time when you feel you have lost the edge of the anointing in your life and are not able to accomplish your job without it. Down in the bottom of the murky river somewhere is your anointing for God's work, but it is lost to you. This is when a spiritual father can help. A perceiving father is a retriever of lost ax heads, lost vision and lost anointing. He will help you find the place where you lost your ax head but it is still your responsibility to pick it up. Ask the Lord to lead you to spiritual parents who are intent on undergirding the next generation of leaders. At the same time, purpose in your heart to become a spiritual parent yourself to the next generation in your life.

God loves to use weak people who only find their strength in Him. You may never feel entirely ready to be a spiritual parent—you just need to be willing.

A new generation of leaders

The Lord is committed to His church. He has promised to return for a church (a bride) that is without spot or wrinkle (Ephesians 5:27). On the day I was married, I looked for my bride at the back of the auditorium, ready to walk the aisle to become my new wife. If she had slipped in the mud a few minutes before her entry, what do you think my reaction would have been? To reject her? Certainly not! I would have done whatever it took to clean her up to prepare her for the wedding!

Our Lord is preparing a bride for Himself. This bride has been soiled and badly wrinkled during the past 2,000 years. But He is committed to cleaning her up to present her to Himself as a glorious church, perfect in every way!

In the last days, the Lord is going to bestow large measures of His Spirit on His people—male and female, young and old:

"And it shall come to pass in the last days, says God, that I will pour out My Spirit on all flesh; your sons and daughters shall prophesy, your young men shall see visions, your old men shall dream dreams. And on My menservants and on My maidservants I will pour out My Spirit in those days; and they shall prophesy" (Acts 2:17-18).

The Lord is committed to raising up a whole new generation of spiritual parents among us. I meet this new breed of leaders week after week as I travel and speak throughout the world. They are marked by *humility* and *servanthood.*

They embrace and honor their spiritual parents who believe in them and coach them. They have no desire to build their own empires. These new leaders see their gifts and anointings as just one of many critical pieces of input needed as they find the mind of Christ together. They honor and lift up other ministries, churches, leaders and believers in their regions. They are secure in their identity and in the Lord's call on their lives as they bless those around them.

Imagine with me for a moment the church in your community in the coming days as she returns to the biblical truth of spiritual parenting. As spiritual parents, our expectation is that the next generation will have a much greater mantle than we have. And not only that, but as the churches in our communities recognize there is no competition in the kingdom of God, but only completion, we will both individually and corporately fulfill the call of God on our lives.

Every gift the Lord has given to us will be properly put to use for the glory of God. And new believers will be birthed into the family of God and nurtured into spiritual parenthood day after day. True family will be restored to the body of Christ.

"Go, find a son"

I like the way Mark Hanby describes a spiritual father:

> A spiritual father is someone whose life and ministry raised you up from the mire of immaturity into proper growth and order. A spiritual father is the one whose words pierced beyond the veneer of a blessing into the very heart and marrow of your existence, causing a massive realignment to your spirit. A spiritual father is not necessarily the one who birthed you into the kingdom. Instead, he is the one who rescues you from the doorstop of your abandonment and receives you into his house, gives you a name, and makes you his son.[1]

God wants to give us a legacy of spiritual sons and daughters but we must connect with them. We must find them and make them our children.

Elijah, the prophet, was discouraged and depressed in I Kings 19. He had just experienced the "high" of the miracle on Mount Carmel, but fled into the desert when he was threatened by the evil Queen Jezebel. There, under a juniper tree, he complained to God of his ill fortune. He was tired, weary, and felt as if he was the only godly man left in the land.

What solution does God give him? "Go, find a son." God believed in Elijah even when he was in the midst of deep depression. Like the good Father He is, God refused to allow Elijah's spiritual legacy to die so easily. Instead, the Lord encouraged him to train a son (Elisha—verse 19) to be his successor. Elijah obeyed, placed his coat on Elisha, and anointed him as his assistant. Once again, he had purpose and direction. His anointing would be multiplied greatly through a son.

As Elijah fathered this spiritual son, one day Elisha asked Elijah for a double portion of the spirit that was on him. I find it interesting that when the Lord took Elijah away to be with Him in the whirlwind, Elisha cried out, "My father, my father," not "My prophet, my prophet" (II Kings 2:12). Elijah had truly become a father to this young prophet.

Elisha experienced a double portion of the Lord's Spirit after being fathered by Elijah. Likewise, we should expect our spiritual children to progress far ahead of us spiritually. True spiritual fathers and mothers live with the expectation that their spiritual sons and daughters will go much further in God than they have ever gone.

Someday, you and I will stand before the Living God. When I stand before the Lord, I do not want to stand there by myself. Let's stand there with a multitude of our spiritual children, grandchildren, and their future descendants! Like Elijah, it's time for you to find a son or daughter! The best is yet to come!

Notes

[1] Dr. Mark Hanby, *You Have Not Many Fathers,* (Shippensburg, Pennsylvania: Destiny Image Publishers, Inc., 1996), p. 94.

Fathering Your Fields

For those called to church leadership

This appendix, concerning fields of ministry and referenced from Chapter 13, gives further clarity to those called to church leadership.

1. What gives a leader authority in his or her field?

One of the spiritual fathers the Lord has placed in my life, Keith Yoder, gives clarity to a church leader's authority in his book, *Healthy Leaders*, when he uses a triangle to illustrate three things that give a leader authority in his field or metron:

> One of the things that gives us authority and releases anointing in our metron is simply the *position* we have—our appointed role as elder, director, overseer, leader, etc. This is one side of the triangle. The position itself carries an anointing to fulfill the responsibility. A second side of the triangle is the aspect of our anointing that comes from the *gifting* we have, whether it be the gift of mercy, the anointing of a pastor or the gift of prophecy. So the *position* we have gives us authority, and the anointing of our *gift* makes a place for us. The third dimension that is most crucial and is the foundation of this triangle is *fellowship* with God. Intimacy, prayer and communion with God releases the anointing within us that brings stability and support to the fact that we are in the leadership position.[1]

2. Why is it important to stay in the right field as a leader?

If you are in the right field, it will yield fruit. A word of caution, however: Just because you have been effective in a certain ministry or in leadership in one part of the world, do not assume you will get the same results at another location. Seek the Lord for His direction. Be sure you are in God's field during each season of your life. God will place you in the proper field where you can be the most effective for Him. He may have to move you to do it! I like how Melody Green stated this same concept: "God is repositioning His players during these days."

I do not mean to imply that we will not face hardship and trials as we obey God in our present field. Sometimes, even if we are in the right place, we will experience times of unfruitfulness. But if the condition persists, we must examine ourselves and our field(s). Our fields should yield fruit.

3. How does God determine and expand our fields as leaders?

Fields of ministry are areas in which God gives us stewardship. It is only the Lord who can determine and expand our fields of ministry. Only He can open up the doors and develop the right fields for us as spiritual leaders (Psalm 75:6-7).

God gave the apostles Paul and Peter different fields to reach in the early days of the church (see Acts, chapters 17-21). Paul's call and anointing was to reach the Gentiles, and Peter's call and anointing was to the Jews.

These lines were so clearly drawn that Paul confronted Peter when Peter crossed over into his field (Galatians 2:11-13). In Antioch, Peter was temporarily helping Paul, but since Peter still carried with him the old notion that Gentiles could not be accepted without circumcision, he allowed his human prejudice toward the uncircumcised Gentiles to undermine what God was doing at Antioch. Paul rebuked Peter for this because he knew God had given him the authority to reach the Gentiles. Peter was interfering in his field.

Later in the scriptures, we see that Peter readjusts his thinking and comes around on the Gentile matter. God had to expand Peter's thinking since his field of ministry was so closely focused on the Jews. Later, Peter speaks favorably of Paul's work (Acts 15:7-11). Through this, I believe Peter learned not to infringe on the ministry field of another, but to submit when he was in their field.

We see many places throughout the New Testament of this kind of submission. Although Paul gave clear oversight to those in his field, when he came to Jerusalem, he submitted to James, the lead apostle in the city. Paul knew he was in James' field (Acts 15). He clearly understood the need to come under authority himself. His field of ministry existed within another field. When fields of ministry coexist in this way, there is unity and respect for each other.

4. How does a leader stay in his field?

As a spiritual leader, you can mentor only those within your sphere of influence—those to whom the Lord has called you. If you stay within your fields of ministry, you will have great authority and confidence. Fields do not limit you but give you great grace to walk within the gifts and calling God has given you.

But if you leave your field, and step into someone else's field and feel you have authority there, you step outside of the grace given to you. Do not presume the anointing and authority you have is a general anointing for you to use anywhere, at any time. This is dangerous, even when done in ignorance. When you move out of your field of calling and anointing, it can open you up to spiritual deception.

Spiritual fathers/leaders will help their spiritual sons stay in their fields. This is a way they can protect them.

Paul understood fields of ministry well. He often appealed to those in authority when he was in their field. In Acts 22:25, he appealed to the Roman guards, stating that in their field he should not be beaten because he was a Roman citizen. So, understanding your field and others' fields may just keep you from getting beaten up by the enemy!

If you recognize the importance of defining your own territory and giving yourself for it, you will avoid infringing on the spiritual territory of another. Work cooperatively and respectfully with existing efforts within your geographical sphere.

Evil powers take advantage when there is confusion or when one intrudes into the field of another. Satan deceiving Adam and Eve in the Garden of Eden is an example of how not everyone who comes into our field is from the Lord. The devil will come to take your field away from you. Stand firm against him with great wisdom and strength.

5. As leaders, let's not tolerate the enemy's activity in our field!

Do not stand for the enemy interfering in your field. Through prayer and intercession and declaring God's Word, rise up in faith and throw the enemy out in Jesus' name! Your God has given you authority in Jesus' name for your field!

In his book, *The House of the Lord,* Francis Frangipane, senior pastor of River of Life Church in Iowa, tells what happened when churches in his city came together in prayer warfare for their city. "Violent crime decreased by 17 percent in Cedar Rapids and FBI files confirm that it became the safest city of more than 100,000 people in the United States. These significant breakthroughs will happen when Christians stand in the gap and take back those areas that the enemy occupies. Satan can only occupy those areas where humanity, through its sin, has allowed him."[2] Christians have the authority to stop the enemy's activity in their field. When spiritual fathers come together to pray regularly in a specific region (their field), the strongholds of the enemy will fall.

During the past few years, pastors have met regularly to pray for our area of Lancaster, Pennsylvania. Recently, on the front page of our local newspaper, I read that crime has dropped 28% in Lancaster city within the past year.[3] Without a doubt, I believe this statistic has a direct correlation to the time spent in unified prayer for Lancaster.

Notes
[1] Keith Yoder, *Healthy Leaders,* (Ephrata, Pennsylvania: House to House Publications, 1998), p. 62.
[2] Francis Frangipane, *The House of the Lord,*(Lake Mary, Florida: Creation House, 1991), p. 56.
[3] Brian Christopher, "City Crime Rate Plummets 28 Percent," *Intelligencer Journal,* September 11, 1999, p. 1.

Fathers Teach Their Sons to Make Decisions

For those called to church leadership

This appendix, to help implement healthy decision-making principles in church government and referenced from Chapter 14, gives further clarity to those called to church leadership.

The early church found itself in a crisis in Acts chapter 15. While they should have been in warfare against the devil's kingdom, they were in a controversy that kept them focusing on this dispute rather than on Christ's kingdom. Does this sound familiar? Church groups today argue over everything from worship service style preferences to the color of the carpet for the sanctuary. But at some point, a decision must be made.

Who makes the decision? How is it made? In Acts 15, we see a model for decision-making in the church. Good leaders will combine the strengths of the three decision-making principles found here. These principles are (1) God speaks through a leader (father), (2) God speaks through a team, and (3) God speaks through His people.

1. A leader who leads the way—episcopal government

God always calls and anoints someone to lead the way and speaks through this spiritual father. James was the head elder and apostle at Jerusalem who held this role.

When a primary leader, called by God, takes his role as the leader of a team and recognizes God speaks through him, this is often called *episcopal government*. Practiced properly, the advantages of this kind of leadership are obvious. Someone needs to take headship of a team, hear what the Lord is saying through the entire team, and make the final decision. Without someone in headship, many situations requiring a final decision would come to an impasse.

Both the Old and New Testament give numerous examples of this "leader who leads the way" leadership principle—Adam, Noah, Abraham, Joseph, Debra, Gideon, David, Jesus, Peter, James, Paul—the list goes on and on. Moses asked the Lord to appoint a man over the congregation in Numbers 27:16. Although Moses worked closely with a leadership team (Aaron and Miriam), he was clearly anointed by God to lead the children of Israel. He knew that someone needed to lead the way after his departure, and Joshua was chosen by the Lord for this responsibility. In the New Testament, in Acts 13:1-4, we read about Barnabas and Saul being sent out with a team as missionaries to evangelize and plant new churches. By verse thirteen, the Bible says Paul and his companions went to the next city. Paul had already become the clear leader—the primary leader of the team.

In many parts of the body of Christ, the primary leader called by God has abdicated his God-given leadership role of authority and responsibility. If God's appointed leader does not lead the way, someone else (who is not God's appointed leader) will fill the leadership vacuum. This opens the door for people to experience confusion and demonic oppression.

A clergy-laity mentality rather than a servant-leader understanding stunts our effectiveness and maintains a distance between church leaders and the rest of the church body. When pastors and other church leaders find themselves leading more like leaders of corporations than fathers, their people will become complacent, seeing no need to actively participate to advance the kingdom of God. Although the primary leader needs to declare a clear vision for the church, he must recognize the importance of helping each person fulfill the call of God on his or her own personal life as a part of that vision.

No matter how scriptural we may believe our leadership style or government to be, if a leader's heart is not that of a servant, there will be problems.

When a church leader leads entirely with this style of decision-making without listening to his team, abuses can occur. That is why it is important to also add the next component of decision-making: working together with a team.

2. God calls a team to work together—presbyerian government

James and the apostles and elders worked as a team to make a decision in Acts 15. The Lord speaking through a team of leaders who discern His voice together is sometimes called *presbyterian government*. We see this team leadership modeled many times in both the Old and New Testament. Leaders rarely worked alone, but with a team of leaders who served with them. Moses and Aaron and Miriam worked together as a team in Exodus. Acts 16:4 speaks of *apostles and elders*, in the plural. In I Peter 5:1, the plural term *elders* is used again. In Titus 1:5, Paul exhorts Titus to appoint elders in every town. Paul and Barnabas appointed elders in every church (Acts 14:23) and worked with them as an eldership team.

The down side to applying this leadership principle only when making decisions is that if a team of elders cannot come to a unanimous decision, the final result could be that no decision is made.

When God called me to start our cell-based church, I had little concept of how to make decisions as a leader. I knew God had called me to start an "underground church," but I did not want to take the reins of the group and lead as a senior pastor. So I insisted that our entire team of leaders, including me, would be coequal. In this way, I thought we could all have a say and would not need a head leader. As I recount in *House to House*:

> It's funny to recall, now, but with six of us leading, we discovered on one Sunday morning that we couldn't come to a decision about who should preach the Word in our celebration meeting. Since none of us were giving clear leadership, no one preached! It would be fine for no one to preach if the Lord was truly leading in this way; however, when it is by default, it causes confusion and stress among the body of Christ. This type of leadership structure will either cause a move of God to stop, or it will slow it down until there is clarity regarding God-

ordained leadership...Within the first year, this "leaderless group" came to the difficult realization that there was a need for clear, delegated leadership among us. Although we continued to believe that team leadership was important, we recognized the need for "headship" on each leadership team.[1]

The abdication of my leadership led to a devastating gridlock when a final decision had to be made. I had to discover that I needed to assume responsibility and receive God's anointing to lead the team, rather than back off and cause the entire church to become frustrated in making decisions.

3. God speaks through His people in the local church— congregational government

The third principle of godly leadership is that God speaks through His people. In Acts 15, James listened to *the people* in the congregation at Jerusalem before he and his team made a final decision.

In Acts 6:1-7, leaders we sometimes call *deacons* were chosen. Who chose the deacons? Scripture says *the people* chose seven men, and the apostles appointed them. Wise leaders will listen to what God says through His people. Leaders must value their people!

It is a godly principle to receive input from those you serve before making a decision that affects them. Before an important decision is made, wise church leaders will publicly share the facts and receive godly input so as to leave no room for doubt and discontent among the congregation.

Some churches rely heavily on the practice of hearing what God's people are saying and then voting on the situation. This is sometimes called *congregational government.* I grew up in a church with this type of church government. We voted on everything from whom the next pastor would be to the type of new pews to order for the church auditorium. The only problem with only applying this type of decision-making is that when you take a vote, someone nearly always loses. Democracy like this works well for civil government where many are unsaved and not listening to the voice of God, but this type of church government alone often is not the best method for making decisions in the church.

The healthy biblical pattern for church government and decision-making is theocracy—God speaking through chosen leaders He has appointed. However, leaders need to recognize that the people of God they are leading are also hearing from the Lord, and they need to honor them by listening and taking into prayerful consideration what the Lord is saying through them.

Biblical decision-making should come through fasting and prayer and spiritual discernment (Acts 13:1-3) involving all three leadership principles. This will bring us balanced decision-making: The leadership team needs to listen to what the Lord is saying through the body. The primary leader listens to what the Lord is saying through the team. Then the primary leader speaks what the Lord is saying, and the others affirm the Lord's direction.

4. How leaders and teams work together to make biblical decisions

In order for biblical decision-making to be effective, the members of the team must be convinced that (1) they are called to serve on the team, (2) others on the team are called with them, and (3) the primary leader is called to serve in his role as the leader of the team. The primary leader must also be fully convinced that every member of the team is called to serve in the role they are in. This is why regular (perhaps yearly) evaluations are so important. It gives everyone the opportunity to express what the Lord is saying to him or her at the present time.

Acknowledge the Lord first. As was mentioned in Chapter 14, the key to all decision-making is simply knowing that only the Lord can give us wisdom for making decisions. We cannot lean on our own understanding as the writer of Proverbs admonishes us in Proverbs 3:5-6: "Trust in the Lord with all your heart, and lean not on your own understanding; in all your ways acknowledge Him, and He shall direct your paths." We must live in the constant reality that Christ is in our midst, waiting for us to ask Him for wisdom and for direction. Jesus tells us clearly in Matthew 18:19-20 (NIV): "Again, I tell you that if two of you on earth agree about anything you ask for, it will be done for you by my Father in heaven. For where two or three come together in my name, there am I with them."

We must continually acknowledge Christ in our midst. Some leadership teams become so familiar with each other they no longer continue to acknowledge the Lord, and they stray from a place of desperation for God and listening to His voice. They are led more by marketing schemes and the latest management style of successful companies. I believe we can learn from the business world, but we need to be sure we are listening to the voice of the Father first and foremost.

Guard our hearts from selfishness. James warns us to guard our hearts from selfish ambition in decision-making in James 3:13-17 (NIV): "Who is wise and understanding among you? Let him show it by his good life, by deeds done in the humility that comes from wisdom. But if you harbor bitter envy and selfish ambition in your hearts, do not boast about it or deny the truth. Such 'wisdom' does not come down from heaven but is earthly, unspiritual, of the devil. For where you have envy and selfish ambition, there you find disorder and every evil practice. But the wisdom that comes from heaven is first of all pure; then peace-loving, considerate, submissive, full of mercy and good fruit, impartial and sincere."

The Lord is concerned that our attitudes be pure before Him so the decisions we make are not based on selfish ambition, which leads to demonic activity in our midst. Many Christian leadership teams have demonic activity, and they are not even aware of it. It is easy to spot. Just look at the fruit. Is there peace, submission, mercy and consideration for the feelings of others, or is there bitterness, envy and selfish ambition? Being right is not the most important issue. Having the Spirit of Christ is the real issue. We can make a bad decision, but if our heart is right, the Lord will direct our paths and turn our bad decision around for good (Romans 8:28).

Avoid the rule of the negative. On a leadership team, the leaders will submit to one another and try to reach a unanimous decision, but this is not always possible. If we were bound by this type of decision-making, in a team of eight, if seven agree and one disagrees, the negative would carry the decision. We can avoid this "rule of the negative," by the spiritual leader of the team being responsible to discern what the Lord is saying through the team and making the final decision within his field of ministry. If a team believes they need unanimity to make a decision, in effect, the dissenting member is leading the team rather than the primary leader.

5. How spiritual fathers provide an outside court of appeal

It is important to note that while we combine the best principles of "a leader leading the way" as he "works through a team" who "listen to those whom they serve" to make decisions, the primary leader and the leadership team should have additional spiritual fathers who provide input and accountability for them. In some denominations, this is the bishop, district superintendent, or denominational leaders. In new apostolic movements, these are the apostolic overseers who serve as spiritual fathers to pastors and to church elders.

Since the primary leader does not have "absolute authority," but "final authority, " there needs always to be a court of appeal. By being accountable even for the final decision, a leader avoids the absolute authority trap. This applies to all levels of leadership.

For example, a small group leader in a local church receives this kind of accountable "outside court of appeal" from his church eldership. The church eldership team receives their outside court of appeal from the apostolic leaders who give them oversight. It is important to note that there needs to be total agreement as to who the fathers are that provide this court of appeal. If there is not complete agreement, in a time of crisis there will not be faith and trust in the court of appeal which is necessary for them to be effective in bringing resolution.

Pastors and churches without an outside court of appeal, will often find a sense of insecurity within their ranks and will try to meet this need by setting up some type of accountability team within the church. This could be a church board, the church elders, a board of deacons, or a pulpit committee. A team like this, within the church providing accountability and oversight for the primary leader of the church, is like young children trying to help their parents through a problem in their marriage by providing accountability for them! They may be sincere, but they simply do not have the grace from the Lord to help their parents. It is not their field of authority or responsibility.

I am grateful to the Lord for a team of spiritual fathers who are outside the DOVE Christian Fellowship International family who speak into my life and into the lives of the other leaders on our international leadership team.

In conclusion

If the natural tendency of a leader is toward the episcopal model of leadership, he needs to trust the Lord for grace to honor his team and listen to the people within his sphere of influence. If the leader's natural tendency is towards the presbyterian model, he needs to be sure he is giving clear leadership during times of crisis or he will frustrate the team. If the leader's personal leadership understanding leans towards the congregational model, he needs to give clear leadership and honor his leadership team by processing decisions in prayer and dialogue with them.

The primary leader often finds his greatest emotional need is *affirmation* from the team members. Elders on a team need to affirm the call of God on their primary leader's life. Assistant cell leaders need to affirm the call on their cell leader's life (I Thessalonians 5:12-13). A wife needs to affirm the call of God on her husband's life (Ephesians 5:33). Those who serve on the team often find their greatest emotional need is for the primary leader to give them *relationship and communication.* Wise leaders will be proactive in "sharing their hearts" with their team. This provides an atmosphere of trust, relationship, openness and security (I Peter 5:1-3).

If you are a church leader, you must understand that without a New Testament church government, you cannot give clear scriptural leadership to the church. Be sure your church constitution and bylaws reflect a New Testament pattern of church government. More instruction on New Testament church government and constitution and by-laws is available in *Helping You Build Cell Churches*, a comprehensive manual for pastors, cell leaders, and church planters (see page 185).

In summary, the team is called by God to support the primary leader. The primary leader protects the team. The primary leader discerns what the Lord is saying through the others on the team. Both the primary leader and the team listen to the wisdom that comes from the people. They are all connected by relationship and accountability. There are fathers to which to appeal, and this brings security to everyone. No one is depending on their own wisdom, but all are trusting the Lord, Who is all Wisdom.

Notes

[1] Larry Kreider, *House to House*, (Ephrata, Pennsylvania: House to House Publications, 1995), pp.6-7.

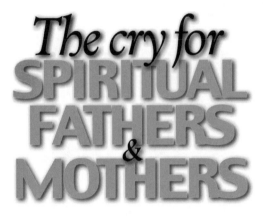

Audio Tape Set
Video Training Set

**For more information about these
resources, check our web site:
www.dcfi.org**

1-800-848-5892

Practical tools for spiritual fathering and mothering

Biblical Foundations

This series of books covers basic Christian doctrine to help a believer grow in Christ. Practical illustrations accompany the easy-to-understand format.

Series Titles

1. Knowing Jesus Christ as Lord
2. The New Way of Living
3. What About Baptisms?
4. Building For Eternity
5. Grace! Grace!
6. Freedom from the Curse
7. Learning to Fellowship with God
8. The Local Church
9. What About Authority and Accountability?
10. God's Perspective on Finances
11. Called to Minister
12. The Great Commission

■ **Small Group Teachings** Each chapter has a teaching outline and questions for group discussion. The twelve book series includes 48 teachings!

■ **Basic Biblical Foundation Course** taught by a Christian leader for a local church.

■ **For a Paul - Timothy Discipleship Relationship** Questions at the end of every chapter can be studied together and life applications discussed.

■ **A Daily Devotional** Each day's reading has corresponding questions at the end of each chapter. The books have four chapters which are each divided into seven days. The set is one year of devotionals.

■ **A Personal Study** of the Bible helps build basic spiritual foundations in the life of every believer.

Each book has 64 pages: **$2.95 each**. Special price for the complete twelve book series: **$29.50**

House To House

How a cell group became an international family of cell-based churches committed to church planting worldwide.

Updated with two new chapters! Today the church is waking up to the simple and successful house to house strategy practiced by the New Testament church 2,000 years ago. *House to House* documents how God called a small fellowship of young believers in Pennsylvania to become an international house to house movement. During the past few years, DOVE Christian Fellowship Int'l has transitioned from a cell-based church into a family of cell-based congregations networking together throughout the world. International Director, Larry Kreider, candidly draws from years of victories and defeats to communicate lessons of operating in a new church paradigm, including:

- How to train cell group leaders
- How to lead a small group
- Reaching the lost through small groups
- How to operate as a leadership team

Use *House to House* as a handbook for cell group dynamics and as a manual to train cell group leaders. Foreword by Dr. Ralph W. Neighbour, Jr.

By Larry Kreider, 206 pages: **$8.95**

Helping You Build Cell Churches Manual

A complete biblical blueprint for cells, this comprehensive 368 page manual covers 54 topics! Gives full, integrated training to build cell churches from the ground up. Includes study and discussion questions. An excellent resource manual for individual or group use: For pastors to train cell leaders, for personal study, to use with DCFI's Cell Ministry Conferences or for presenting a *Helping You Build Seminar* at your church. For more about this affordable tailor-made seminar for your church using this manual, check our web site: www.dcfi.org

Compiled by Brian Sauder and Larry Kreider, 368 pages: $19.95 **20% discount** for ten or more books.

Manual topics cover:

▲ Cell leadership training
▲ Healthy cell life
▲ Reaching out
▲ Mistakes to avoid
▲ Church government
▲ Fivefold ministry in cells
▲ Children and youth in cells
▲ Church planting
▲ Transitioning to a cell-based church
▲ Counseling skills for cell leaders
▲ and much more!

The Tithe: A Test in Trust

This book answers key questions about tithing based on the scriptures, explaining it as both an Old Testament and a New Testament teaching. Written with a variety of illustrations, this book has been used to help believers understand that the tithe is a test in trust—trust in God and trust in our spiritual leadership. By Larry Kreider. 32 pages: **$2.95**

Growing Healthy Cell Groups Seminar

This dynamic seminar offers field-tested training
to help you grow effective cell groups.
For pastors and cell leaders.

Youth Cells Ministry Seminar

Learn the values behind youth cells so cell ministry does not
become just another program at your church.
For adult and teen leaders!

Church Planting Clinic

A clinic designed to help you formulate a successful
strategy for cell-based church planting.
For those involved in church planting and those considering it.

Small Group Leader's Counseling Basics Seminar

This seminar takes you through the basics of counseling,
specifically in small group ministry.
Includes a comprehensive manual.

Fivefold Ministry Seminar

A conference designed to release healthy, effective fivefold
ministry in the local church. For fivefold ministers and pastors
who want to see the fivefold ministry released.

Call for complete brochures
1-800-848-5892

For dates, locations and details check our web site:
www.dcfi.org   email: dcfi@dcfi.org